The Institute for Learning and Teaching in Higher Education

Institutions, academics and the assessment of prior experiential learning

Norman Evans

with a Foreword by
Lord Ron Dearing
Chairman of the Committee of Inquiry into
Higher Education, 1996–1997

London and New York

First published 2001 by RoutledgeFalmer
11 New Fetter Lane, London EC4P 4EE

Simultaneously published in the USA and Canada
by RoutledgeFalmer
29 West 35th Street, New York, NY 10001

RoutledgeFalmer is an imprint of the Taylor & Francis Group

Typeset in Sabon by BC Typesetting, Bristol
Printed and bound in Great Britain by
TJ International Ltd, Padstow, Cornwall

British Library Cataloguing in Publication Data
A catalogue record for this book is available from the British Library

Library of Congress Cataloging in Publication Data
Evans, Norman, 1923–
    The Institute for Learning and Teaching in Higher Education:
    institutions, academics, and the assessment of prior experiential
    learning/Norman Evans; with a foreword by Lord Ron Dearing.
        p. cm.
    Includes bibliographical references and index.
    1. Institute for Learning and Teaching in Higher Education
    (Great Britain) 2. Higher education and state–Great Britain.
    3. College teachers–Great Britain–Societies, etc. I. Title.

LC178.G7 E93 2001
378.1′25′0941–dc21   00-068360

ISBN 0–415–24002–6

Contents

Foreword

No students, no universities, no colleges.

And yet historically, the road to academic acclaim, financial reward and preferment has not lain through excellence in the practice of teaching or the management of learning, but through achievement in research. As someone put it to the Review Committee I chaired to advise on the future development of higher education in the UK: 'Staff talk of the teaching load and the research opportunity'.

There has been a disjunction between the rewards system for faculty and the needs of the student. Some years ago, as the Chairman of the Funding Council for Higher Education in England, I put it to the vice-chancellors that they led the only profession I could recall that does not cherish and develop its professionalism through a professional institute, an institute owned not by employers but by the members of the profession. That thought remained with me during the work of the Review Committee and was reflected in the recommendation for the creation of an Institute for Learning in Higher Education. Alongside that we also recommended that the profession of teaching should rank equally with research in the rewards system. Without that reality not much would happen.

A Foreword is not the place for a development of the arguments, but since this book is concerned with the assessment of prior learning as well as with the Institute, it is relevant to add that assessment is central to the professionalism of the teacher, and the challenge is most obvious in the assessment of prior learning, both in terms of equity for the student and the safeguarding of the standing of awards. A student can escape a poor teacher, but not a bad marker, who is not only a threat to the student, but to the credibility of the rewards system itself. In a society committed to the practice of Lifelong Learning we must recognise prior learning and develop the techniques for its assessment.

Finally, a word to the academic concerned with academic freedom. The Institute is not about putting Government of Funding Council controls. It is about the profession itself taking responsibility for raising the standards and standing of its own central professionalism and getting proper recognition for achievement in a way which has been denied by the rewards system in the past.

Lord Ron Dearing
Chairman of the National Committee of Inquiry into
Higher Education
2000

Preface

Many will say that it is far too soon to be writing a book about the Institute for Learning and Teaching in Higher Education (ILTHE). Without clear evidence of achievements or deficiencies, comment is bound to be premature and superficial. In some senses of course that is correct. There is no detailed analysis here of any aspect of its work. But this book does not set out to conduct an evaluation of ILTHE performance. Rather it is to try to catch it on the wing, identifying its origin and gestation, offering some comments on the issues which will face institutions and individuals if and when they choose to use the facility of the assessment of prior experiential learning, and probing the potential of the ILTHE for becoming an influential player in the higher education of the future, through contributing to the enhancement of students' learning.

Like all developments in education, that is bound to be controversial. It is particularly so at a time of high tensions between government and institutions which get exposed in issues of funding, the increasing number of ring-fenced activities, programme development with government intervention to put heavy emphasis on employability and raising fears about a nasty creep towards a national curriculum, quality assurance and all the to-do about accountability and transparency, much of which gets rounded up in the overall unresolved issue of central control versus institutional autonomy. The quasi-nationalisation of higher education has gone far enough, so it is said. Too far, say others. It was abandoned for coal, steel, electricity, gas, transport and water, so why should it continue for higher education when it is utterly inappropriate for anything to do with knowledge, let alone its extension. Others claim that in the interests of social justice, extending access and widening participation there needs to be strong national intervention, so given some financial tweaking to improve funding, the system will be able to serve all sections of the population as it should.

As a professional membership organisation that is the context in which the ILTHE has to find its way. How it finds its way, how far it will emerge with membership being the 'norm' for academics in higher education indicating a competence in teachers as Dearing envisaged it, with research promoted and made available as a national facility, or how far it will be more than that, time alone will tell. This book is merely a contribution to the debate about the where, what and how of the part which the ILTHE (colloquially known as the ILT) might be able to play in the future.

Acknowledgements

No-one can write a book like this without a great deal of help from many people. Those who have helped in this effort are too many to mention by name. Let me just say that without the perspectives offered by some very experienced staff and education developers, the effort would have been greatly the poorer.

Three people though must be mentioned, for they read and commented on the manuscript, offering invaluable insights and suggesting changes in emphasis.

Malcolm Barry, Director of Continuing Education and Head of Professional and Community Education at Goldsmiths College, University of London, gave particularly valuable comments at various stages of the preparation of the document.

Anne Rumpus, Head of the Education Initiative Centre at the University of Westminster, read the full script and commented from her long experience of promoting staff development and introducing AP(E)L to her institution.

Morris Keeton contributed yet again, using his American eyes and sharp philosophical approach to see how far the story of this new development in the UK made sense to an interested observer.

The comments were theirs. And deficiencies are mine.

Abbreviations

AP(E)L	Assessment of Prior and Experiential Learning
AUT	Association of University Teachers
BSA	Basic Skills Agency
CAEL	Cooperative Assessment of Experiential Learning, then Council for the Advancement of Experiential Learning, and now Council for Adult and Experiential Learning
CATS	Credit Accumulation Transfer Service
CPD	Continuing Professional Development
CNAA	Council for National Academic Awards
CVCP	Committee of Vice Chancellors and Principals, now Universities UK
DE	Department of Employment
DfEE	Department of Education and Employment
ETS	Education Testing Service
FIPSE	Fund for the Improvement of Post Secondary Education
FEU	Further Education Unit
GLTC	Generic Learning and Teaching Centre
ILTHE	Institute of Learning and Teaching in Higher Education
ILT	Institute of Learning and Teaching – shortened version of the ILTHE
ILEA	Inner London Education Authority
LTSN	Learning and Teaching Support Network
HEI	Higher Education Institution
HEQC	Higher Education Quality Council
MEd	Master Of Education
OECD	Organisation for Economic and Cooperative Development
NCIHE	National Committee of Inquiry into Higher Education
NCVQ	National Council for Vocational Qualifications
PGCW	Postgraduate Certificate of Education

PSI	Policy Studies Institute
QAA	Quality Assurance Agency
SEDA	Staff and Educational Development Association
THETO	The Higher Education Training Organisation
WBL	Work Based Learning
UCoSDA	Universities and College Staff Development Agency

Introduction

Implementing the Vision.
Enhancing the status of teaching.
Improving the experience of teachers.
Supporting innovation in higher education.

That is the banner headline which greets anyone who looks at the Website of the Institute for Learning and Teaching for Higher Education in the year 2000. Things have moved along quite steadily for an educational enterprise since the Dearing Committee made the recommendation in its report from the National Committee of Inquiry into Higher Education (NCIHE) in July 1997 that such an Institute be established. Its intention was clear: to promote the enhancement of learning and teaching of students up the academic agenda to begin to move towards parity with research attainments.

The NCIHE was set up by the Tory government with support from the then Labour Opposition essentially to try to find ways of getting the money necessary to sustain the higher education system because tax monies available were proving not only inadequate but positively damagingly so. Inevitably such an inquiry led to all manner of matters concerning universities and colleges. One of those was staff development and hence the recommendation for the ILT. By 1997 when the Report was submitted, Labour was in power as government and among other recommendations which it accepted was that for the ILT.

The Committee's clarion cry for the recommendation was:

It should become the norm for all permanent staff with teaching responsibilities to be trained on an accredited course.

(para 70)

In the light of that proclamation and the ILT's three-part vision this book has four purposes. Each supports the others. And in one way and another all concern students' learning. The first is to provide the background story to the evolution and establishment of the Institute for Learning and Teaching in Higher Education in Britain. The second is to document the central role played by the assessment of prior experiential and learning (AP(E)L) in the thinking and planning which led to the ILT and now features in its day-to-day work. One without the other produces an unintelligible story. Missing a wheel or two. Together they amount to a pair of developments which are unique in the world. Nowhere else is there anything comparable to the establishment with government backing of a national institution whose sole purpose, as a voluntary, membership, professional organisation, is to enhance the quality of learning and teaching throughout the system of higher education. Equally, in no other country is there any professional association which, because of its commitment, offers strong inducement for academics to develop AP(E)L schemes for themselves, whether or not such facilities are open to students in their institutions. The third purpose is to attempt to give some support to those institutions and individuals who are moving to engage with the ILT and in particular considering going down the AP(E)L route for the first time, with some do's and don'ts based on the experience of the last nearly twenty years of helping its evolution in the system in the UK and elsewhere, watching its ups and downs.

And that points to the fourth purpose. It is to speculate on the possible consequences of the first three related purposes. The Institute for Learning and Teaching and the central and explicit use of AP(E)L are growing up in tandem at the very time when government policies are taking yet more twists and turns to current practice in attempts to extend access further, to promote Lifelong Learning, essentially on economic grounds, and widening participation to enhance the employability of as many people as possible in this new knowledge dominated world. The Foundation degree is merely the latest initiative to promote all that. This certainly means bringing into the system more men and women who have gained a good deal of knowledge from their experience of employment and life. They will not be older versions of the traditional school leaver entrant. What is unknowable at present is how far using AP(E)L techniques for their own purposes of acquiring membership of the ILT will affect academics' teaching stance and personal attitudes to students, in ways which will implicitly service government's wider purposes.

It is almost as if the Dearing Committee, having made a recommendation for a new institution and had it accepted by universities and colleges as well as government, because of the AP(E)L component which has been incorporated additionally has been instrumental in promoting a staff development programme which accords with government policy and aspiration. Work-based learning is central to those government efforts. That is just another way of talking about AP(E)L. So, if it follows its vision the ILT could find itself following an unwritten part of its script; promoting a quiet evolution in curricula and provision. Blue sky dreaming can even imagine that to be an influence every bit as potent for higher education generally as the more public shifts effected by government, say as turning polytechnics into universities, which was more than some deft name changes, or introducing student tuition fees, or even showing a thing or two about student learning to the Quality Assurance Agency. Could, not will.

How far that quiet evolution runs depends in part on how academics and their institutions react to the arrival of AP(E)L as part of their mainstream activity. If the ILT means what it says – supporting innovation in higher education – it could turn out to be a rather different institution from what many assumed it would be.

There is another sense in which the ILT when properly established may differ from expectations. This is because Dearing's recommendation can be read in a different way. Intentionally or not, and despite the Committee's careful insistence that the ILT should be a 'hands off' body, it can be seen as yet another step towards increasing still more the centralisation of the system as a whole. As a membership professional organisation therefore the ILT will have to position itself somewhere along the line which runs from centralisation to institutional autonomy. That may seem light years away from membership of the ILT becoming the 'norm' for academic staff in higher education. But it is more than likely that the ILT will find itself caught up in the unresolved tensions between the need for higher education to be publicly accountable with the means of doing so and institutions' need to have time and space to be able to fulfil their prime academic responsibilities and innovate as their own circumstances may dictate.

Institutional change – that's the name of the game. Behind all the rhetoric, whether for the ILT, Lifelong Learning, the Foundation degree, the employability of newly qualified graduates, widening access and increasing participation, quality assurance and benchmarking, lies the same dilemma. How do institutions created for one set of purposes change to respond to a different set of purposes in changing circumstances? One way or another everything speaks of institutional change. And the point of it all is to enhance student learning without damaging the vital research role of universities. So the most intriguing question about the ILT is where, how, and if at all, it makes a contribution to those searching national questions.

The first purpose is covered in Chapters 1 and 2, which tell the story between spring 1997 and 2000 of the origins, genesis and early operation of the ILT. To make sense of the second purpose there is a brief account in Chapter 3 of the evolution of AP(E)L in Britain from 1980. Some of the difficulties it can pose for individual academics and institutions come in Chapter 4.

Chapter 5 takes the ILT 's approach to accreditation as its starting point, sets it alongside the programme requirements for approval by the Staff and Educational Development Association (SEDA), and Chapter 6 attempts to give an indication of some of the different flavours there are to accredited courses, as institutions evolve their own schemes. Chapter 7 plots the different pathways open for individuals to become members of the ILT and comments on them. Chapter 8 is about the fast track towards membership.

Chapter 9 considers Continuing Professional Development (CPD) as the means of remaining in good standing with the ILT and its implications for individuals, institutions and for the ILT itself, where CPD has to be of pivotal significance.

Chapter 10 then speculates on what might be some of the consequences of this double-pronged initiative, the ILT itself and AP(E)L within it. One thing seems certain. Whatever its explicit purpose, the twin initiatives of establishing the ILT and incorporating AP(E)L in its official procedures, implicitly has launched an engine with huge potential for stimulating an academic staff development programme which brings academics nearer to their students' own learning experience, with clues as to how it can be enhanced and extended. Add in the establishment of the twenty centres making up the development end of the Learning and Teaching Support Network (LTSN) and the Generic Learning and Teaching Centre (GLTC) and the point is underlined. All that sits in the muddied context of institutional change.

So, at this juncture there is a vast expansion of learning opportunities arising from changes in the economic, domestic and social world, not to speak of the communications revolution. There is an unparalleled series of overlapping attempts to assist individual academics and institutions to come to terms with what that expansion means in opportunities for students to learn. At best, if it can realise its three-part vision the ILT can be seen as a broker for helping to arrange the best fit between these two entities to help create a higher education fit for the twenty-first century. At worst it will sit on the sidelines as a professional membership organisation with its members and the CPD requirements to remain in good standing, but with its bold vision in tatters. The ILT is a professional membership association. It will become what its members want it to become.

1 Beginnings

The assessment of prior experiential learning (AP(E)L) is one of the fascinations of the story about the Institute for Learning and Teaching in Higher Education (ILT) in Britain. Both the Institute itself and AP(E)L in its context are unique in the world.

Amidst all the discussions worldwide, about the quality of learning and teaching in higher education, Great Britain stands alone in inventing a national body to promote that quality. Its underlying purpose is to improve students' learning, foster self-directed learning and enable staff themselves to follow a route to be recommended to their own students. Not that it is a legal requirement (yet) for universities and colleges to have anything to do with this new body, but the pressures are there from government for all institutions to make arrangements for their academics to become members of the new body, and to persuade, cajole, maybe require them to secure membership of what has been established in April 1999 as the Institute of Learning and Teaching in Higher Education (also abbreviated as the ILT). It is unique.

It is also unique in a worldwide context in including in its provision the assessment of prior and experiential learning (AP(E)L). That means it becomes an institutional mainstream activity for academic staff themselves. As the story unfolds it will be seen that backed by this new academic body, AP(E)L can become a facility available to academics in all universities and colleges irrespective of their standing and whether or not AP(E)L services are available for students. That seems incredible when its implications are thought through; AP(E)L for academics whether or not they engage in it with their students.

It is also vital throughout this story to hold in mind that the Institute is there to serve learning support staff as well as fully fledged academics. That means that librarians, information technology staff, laboratory assistants, part-time staff, postgraduate students who also teach, all could seek membership provided that their contributions to the academic work of the Institution merited it. AP(E)L could well be vital for many of them in seeking membership.

It was the National Committee of Inquiry into Higher Education's (NCIHE) Report in July 1997 which recommended the establishment of an Institute of Learning and Teaching. Recommendation 13 reads:

> We recommend that institutions of higher education begin immediately to develop or seek access to programmes of teacher training for their staff if they do not have them, and that all institutions seek national accreditation of such programmes from the Institute of Learning and Teaching for Higher Education.
>
> (ILT)

Recommendation 14 introduced an essential condition. It was for representative bodies in consultation with the Funding Councils to establish the ILT. This recommendation was a vital caveat. It was smoothing the way for acceptance of the recommendation by higher education. As such it was in line with the long-standing device of government employing what can be claimed as a hands-off approach to something it wanted to achieve. As a membership organisation higher education institutions themselves would own the ILT, through their academics memberships, while government retained its influence through the Funding Councils having a seat on its board as of right. Money talks!

The NCIHE's reasoning for the recommendations were given in paragraph 8.76. It was to:

> raise the status of teaching across higher education, help the UK to become world leader in the practice of teaching at higher levels, and emphasise the importance of learning. This should be a national objective to enable the UK to compete effectively in the next century in a world where the quality, relevance and effectiveness of education and training systems will underpin future prosperity.

The Committee of Inquiry itself was established by the Tory government, true in close consultation with the Labour Opposition, but essentially to try to find an answer to the vexed question of how best to fund the higher education system. At that time there was general agreement that it was being endangered. It had succeeded almost beyond all rational expectations in expanding student numbers. It had done so while the per capita funding was actually reduced. Between 1984 and 1998 numbers had risen by 35% while the funding for each student dropped by 36% between 1989 and 1997. There were no more so-called efficiency gains to be squeezed from budgets to bolster institutional finances. There was a funding crisis. The Tory government funked it. It avoided taking the decision which the incoming Labour government in May 1997 took when it received the Committee's report in July 1997; student tuition fees would be levied in future and maintenance allowances scrapped, all to be replaced with a student loan scheme, with a raft of exemptions necessary to protect those who could not afford such fees. This was not an exact version of Dearing's recommendation of how students should bear some of the costs of their higher education. But the principle was grasped. Public money for higher education had to be supplemented from somewhere and part of that somewhere had to be students. And with it the redistributive principle was upheld. It was a move to correct the long-standing and unacceptable fact that one section of the population was being supported in higher education in part by tax monies from those with the lowest incomes. This injustice as many see it was worsened by the general tendency for the gap to widen between the incomes of graduates and those of non-graduates.

But charging fees immediately raised questions about value for money in a completely different way for higher education. Employers had long since raised complaining voices that the newly graduated men and women they took on as employees needed additional training before they were fit for the job to which they had been appointed. They went further. They questioned the nature of the curriculum as a preparation for employment. They queried the quality of the teaching which students received. But now with fees to pay, students too would press those same questions about the quality of the service they were receiving.

All that was part of a long-standing argument between higher education and government about what academic staff actually did for their salaries. This was a loaded argument because both sides knew that there were plenty of examples of idle, lazy or even incompetent academic staff who fulfilled neither their research obligations nor properly their responsibilities as teachers of students, despite the fact that the vast majority of academics were thoroughly committed to their posts. The unhappy result of this kind of public slanging match was that the recognition was never given to the staff who alone made that expansion possible.

The research part of the equation was brought into sharp focus as the Funding Councils devised ways of conducting Research Assessments of the research actually undertaken by each higher education institution and used the results of those assessments to weight the annual sums disbursed to universities and colleges. Naturally, this tended to concentrate the attention of all academics and their senior colleagues on producing evidence of research activities. Naturally too, this raised anxieties on the part of many in the system, that undue attention to research inevitably risked by accident or design demoting teaching as a less valuable activity and diminishing its quality. The introduction of a Teaching Assessment exercise to run parallel with the research inquiries did something to tilt the balance back towards looking for excellence in teaching. How far excellent teaching results in enhanced learning by students is another matter. But research remained the weightier factor.

In part, therefore, the Dearing recommendation for the establishment of an Institute of Learning and Teaching can be seen as a response to all those variegated pressures. Alongside its attempt to find ways of creating an alternative financial regime to combat the funding problems of the higher education system, clearly it sought to help institutions find ways of improving the quality of teaching as a counterbalance to the weight which had been placed on research. At the same time, by establishing a new professional body it sought to heighten the status of teaching in higher education alongside that accorded to research. This was all the more important because the full title of the report was Higher Education in the Learning Society. Throughout there were implications for higher education in promoting Lifelong Learning. But if higher education was to make its proper contribution to that concept – Lifelong Learning in a learning society – it was obvious that it would need to pay close attention to its approaches to learning and teaching, especially of older students. Older students are not older versions of 18-plus students. They are different and much of higher education has a good deal to learn about what those differences mean for learning and teaching.

Beyond that too, the heavy emphasis in explaining the recommendation on the need for the UK to sustain its academic reputation in the global knowledge market, highlighted the need for higher education to tend its laurels rather than rest on them. So the Institute for Learning and Teaching in Higher Education is no trendy piece of window dressing for the system. It is deadly serious business.

However, long before the Dearing Committee made its recommendation, there were other bodies, not to mention universities and colleges, which took just as seriously, and some would argue more professionally, the need to try to enhance the sheer professionalism of teaching in higher education. The Universities and Colleges Staff Development Agency (UCoSDA) was started by the Committee of Vice Chancellors and Principals (CVCP) in 1988 with a certain amount of prodding from government. This was to be the universities' engine for academic staff development. In 1990 the CVCP set up its Academic Audit Unit, again under some pressure from government. Both were flying early warning signs to the system that Whitehall was beginning to conduct a rather more detailed scrutiny of what universities were actually doing. And both were responses of the CVCP to those pressures in an effort to demonstrate that universities were not only able to tackle the questions of quality which implicitly government was questioning, but to do so in an open, transparent way. Unfortunately, the CVCP never gave to UCoSDA the same strong support it gave to its Audit Unit, so that the potential for staff development was never exploited. Funding problems produced a contractual relationship between UCoSDA and the Department of Employment, an arrangement which did not recommend itself to much of the system. It smacked of government intervention which was both resisted and resented.

At this point it is instructive to note that from 1987 to 1988 Ron Dearing was chairman of the Council for National Academic Awards, the academic authority for all degrees and diplomas taught outside the universities. He was also chair on the Polytechnics and Colleges Funding Council from 1988 to 1993, chair of the Universities Funding Council from 1991 to 1993 and chair of the Higher Education Funding Council for England from 1992 to 1993. His views about staff development in higher education were those of a thoroughly well-informed insider.

However, in the public sector as then was, colleges and polytechnics had long had the Standing Conference on Educational Development (SCED). This was a voluntary organisation with no official institutional standing, composed of individuals who were committed to the concept of staff development. Nor were those two bodies, UCoSDA and SCED, the only ones to take a close interest in staff development. The Society for Research in Higher Education (SRHE) had a group of members which, like SCED, were concerned to promote ideas about staff development throughout the system. The time was when that group felt it lacked adequate support from the SRHE and so it negotiated a merger with SCED to create the Staff and Educational Development Association (SEDA). SEDA then had the idea of promoting a scheme which would raise the profile of education development in general and in particular the proficiency of teachers in higher education. To this end it developed an Accreditation of Teachers in Higher Education Scheme (ATHES). In 1991 it was launched as a pilot exercise. It proved successful and the Scheme was launched nationally in 1993. Like the pilot, this was successful nationally. By 1997 when Dearing began sitting, some seventy institutions had their programmes recognised by SEDA and more were waiting approval, some of which were overseas. By then it had some 2000 academic staff who had met its requirements for accreditation.

And then there was the Association of University Teachers (AUT), which kept an ear to the ground about these matters in the interests of its members. This meant that there were three interested groups committed to the overall concept of staff development in higher education long before the Tories thought up the idea of using the Dearing Committee as an escape route from facing up to the problems of financing the expanded system which they had promoted.

Putting UCoSDA, SEDA and the AUT together amounted to a solid commitment within higher education to staff development across institutions for improving learning and teaching by the mid-1990s. Indeed it would have been hard to find a university or college which did not by that time have some sort of programme to advance the professionalism of its academic staff. There were education development units and centres for education initiative in all parts of the country. But like many initiatives in education at any level, in no sense was it systematic and inevitably was bound to be patchy. It all meant, however, that when Dearing produced the recommendation for an Institute of Learning and Teaching, in many ways it was pushing against an open door.

That is not to say there were no problems. Perhaps the largest was another body in the field which had caused much anxiety on higher education since its establishment in 1986 – the National Council for Vocational Qualifications (NCVQ). This was a new body introduced to create some coherence among the myriad organisations which offered vocational qualifications that hundreds of thousands of students in further education took every year. With differing levels of success, it tried to do so by using a competence model of achievement, based on functional analysis, with a yes/no assessment system. This seemed perilously near to introducing behavioural objectives as a template for designing curricula. Philosophically this was antipathetic to higher education's views of itself, and indeed brought into play a vigorous argument about the differences between vocational training and education. The NCVQ had from its beginning the intention and ambition to apply its vocational approach to every level of higher education awards. Hence higher education's anxieties.

So when it was known well in advance of the publication of the Dearing Report that there would be a recommendation to establish an Institute for Learning and Teaching, both SEDA and the AUT sought to take the initiative, knowing full well how, given a chance, the NCVQ, and the then to be established Quality Assurance Agency as a successor to the Higher Education Quality Council would attempt to make the running for the new Institute. Some would say they looked for a pre-emptive strike. Together they approached Professor Clive Booth, recently retired as Vice Chancellor of Oxford Brookes University and as Vice Chairman of the CVCP. They sought him out as a trusted honest broker, to chair a group convened through the CVCP to think through some of the implications of the yet to be recommended ILT. Given the experience of universities with other government-inspired initiatives of the Quality Assurance Agency and the Funding Council concerning criteria for assessing the effectiveness of both teaching and research, it was clearly in the interests of the CVCP to develop is own proposals for the ILT rather than wait to see what other suggestions might appear.

Hence it was in anticipation of the Dearing recommendations that the Committee of Vice Chancellors and Principals (CVCP) convened an Accreditation and Teaching in Higher Education: Planning Group. Fourteen national bodies were represented in that group (see membership list in Appendix 1) to produce a design for the new Institute. Beginning work in June 1997 it commissioned a paper by an outside consultant which went out for comments from institutions in October 1997. Among other findings the investigation confirmed that there was a substantial amount of staff development but that, unsurprisingly, its institutional and geographical coverage was patchy. A second consultation document, composed in the light of the seventy-five responses received to the first, was sent out in January 1998 with a series of questions to which answers were asked for by March 1998.

That consultation document outlined the group's ideas for the purpose of the ILT. It was, they said:

- to enhance the status of teaching in higher education;
- to maintain and improve the quality of learning and teaching in higher education;

• to set standards of good professional practice that its members, and in due course, all those with teaching and learning responsibilities in higher education might follow.

It raised the question as to what, if any, connection there should be between membership of the Institute and the probation of newly appointed tutors; and further whether membership should constitute a licence to practice. Unsurprisingly, when those questions were put out for discussion, both where rejected firmly. It also raised questions about possible relationships with other professional bodies and the long-standing subject groups organised by specialist academics themselves.

The document included a draft of a national statement as a basis for planning programmes for the accreditation referred to in the Dearing recommendation.

This is where AP(E)L makes its surprising, and as it turned out, definitive entry. It also offered a detailed illustration of how routes to membership might work as a catalyst for further discussion. The paper was at pains to ensure adequate arrangements for experienced staff to achieve membership should they want it. Paragraph 1.18 says:

> Individuals would achieve professional membership of the Institute having successfully met the requirements of an accredited programme or pathway. These could be work-based, course-based, involve one-to-one mentoring, distance and open learning, the assessment of prior (experiential) learning AP(E)L, or various combinations of those or other modes.

It would be hard to imagine a more comprehensive set of possible routes to membership, just as in advance it is difficult to have foreseen that AP(E)L was to appear as a recommended means of seeking membership.

The paper went on to emphasise the need to meet the requirements of experienced staff and to be sensitive to the position of academic staff who might find themselves moving from one institution to another. Paragraph 1.19 went on:

> It will be important to enable staff to gain membership of the Institute wholly or partly by way of their demonstrable experience and qualifications and to cater for people moving from one HEI to another whilst following an accredited programme. One way

of doing this would be to draw on and adapt as necessary the experience of schemes of assessment that recognise individuals prior experience and learning. Some of the schemes are known by the term 'accreditation of prior (experiential)' learning (AP(E)L), but this is using the word accreditation differently from its use in the present paper. However, the AP(E)L approach deserves very serious consideration as one possible pathway.

So, right from the beginning AP(E)L was there at the forefront of thinking about what membership of the Institute of Learning and Teaching meant for experienced academics.

The paper sketched the possible categories of membership of the new body; Part One Associateship, Part Two Associateship, Membership and Fellowship. For each level it sketched an illustrative hierarchy of responsibilities running through classroom practice, module design – including an assessment scheme and an evaluation scheme – curriculum design, including the preceding elements, and leadership in change whether in teaching or curricula, through research, publication, work with disciplinary or professional bodies. For each level and category it outlined in tabular form what members might be expected to know and do as evidence that they had met successfully the relevant set of learning outcomes. For illustration, it set out the categories of underpinning knowledge and professional values underpinning practice. And at some length it spelled out the curriculum for what this would mean in practice (see tables in Appendix 3 and 4).

The Executive Summary of the draft prospectus for the ILT was among the papers for the CVCP meeting in January 1998. It indicated that 95% of the 178 responses accepted the need for a national accreditation scheme and that 77% supported the approach of the Booth group. In accepting it every HEI in the land was endorsing, either explicitly or implicitly, that AP(E)L was a publicly recognised mainstream academic activity suitable for enabling their own academic staff to seek membership of the new body.

Paragraph 10 reads:

> Membership for existing staff would be available via a range of routes, including advanced standing and the accreditation of prior (experiential) learning.

This paper went out for a second consultation between January and March 1998. There were 178 responses, comprising 117 from HEIs,

42 from associations and national bodies, and the rest from individuals: 95% accepted the need for a national accreditation scheme and 77% endorsed the general approach taken by the Booth group. One question which asked about routes to membership was:

> Is the approach of accrediting a wide range of programmes and pathways, including AP(E)L, practicable? Will this give sufficient scope for institutions to devise their own solutions to meeting the national statement in their own way?

Answers showed a general agreement that it did. The usual worries about the difficulties posed by AP(E)L were referred to: cost, time taken, and so on. But most emphasis was put on the need for training in those institutions without experience of AP(E)L because 'it was recognised that internal assessors would have to be trained and that procedures would need to be well-structured, rigorous and fair. AP(EL) should not be seen as a soft option, an easy route to membership.' It was suggested that in due course the Institute should draw up guidelines on AP(E)L. It was also suggested in some responses that 'no pathway should be based on AP(E)L alone', emphasis being put on 'the sharing of experience and ideas with others similarly placed'.

Both the Consultation paper and the responses to it made it abundantly clear that, if such a service were to be available for existing staff, each of the 167 institutions on the Funding Council's list has to have available either their own staff developers and internal AP(E)L assessors who had been trained for the purpose, or access to those facilities in another institution. This was of fundamental importance. The ILT needed to reach a critical mass of membership as soon as possible to give it creditability. To facilitate that there had to be some version of AP(E)L available for those experienced staff to seek and secure membership. Indeed it needed to be available to help persuade experienced academics to seek membership in the first place. Formal taught courses and sitting in classrooms was hardly going to attract them. And if, as seems likely, in the future, the Funding Council takes account of numbers and levels of membership when making decisions about an institution's funding, there will be strong incentives to do so. So, getting institutions up to speed on AP(E)L has become essential unless an institution formed a partnership with another which has already the expertise and experience required.

At the time of the Consultation and the polling of institutions for their ideas, there was no reliable information nationally about the numbers of universities and colleges which were practising AP(E)L let alone a directory of them. At that time guesswork suggested there were about 100-plus which had no experience of AP(E)L and about 40 which had.

Since then the Learning from Experience Trust (LET) has completed a survey, funded by the Department for Education and Employment, of AP(E)L activities throughout the higher education system in England – funding did not run to covering Scotland, Wales and Northern Ireland – so that there is now a database available to show how many, of what kind and whereabouts in the country universities and colleges are actually using AP(E)L techniques. It is called 'Changing but not Changed' and is referred to in greater detail in the next chapter.

The papers suggested three different levels of membership. Paragraph 9:

> Associateship: where a member is associated with the profession, but not a full practising member.
> Junior membership: where these members are progressing towards full membership.
> Membership: upon completion of an accredited programme/ pathway for those practising the profession.

As for timing, Paragraph 22 of the CVCP Consultation document says that the ILT will be established as a company in the autumn of 1998 and officially launched in the spring of 1999. This is the earliest date that the ILT would be in a position to provide comprehensive information on its services, including a publication and a Website; recruit members and provide them with a professional service; begin accreditation of institutional programmes/pathways.

And with that the Booth group's work was done. The results of that consultation produced a final report in May 1998. It ended with a set of recommendations to be taken up by its successor, The Institute for Learning and Teaching Planning Group. Among those recommendations was one suggesting the importance of establishing a 'fast track' towards membership for experienced practitioners. It was difficult to imagine how such a scheme could be developed without using AP(E)L.

All in all, through the Booth group the CVCP had taken a firm grip on what an Institute of Learning and Teaching ought to look like in the event of such a recommendation being made.

However, there is an interesting and maybe instructive omission in its work. The emphasis on the need to incorporate AP(E)L in the ILT's provision concentrates on it as a process for achieving membership.

In doing so implicitly it is making assumptions about the validity of reflection on experience as a source of assessable academic learning. That is not explicit but it has to be the case. By contrast there are no such pedagogical implications to be drawn from any other of its recommendations. The Booth group took considerable trouble to draft a set of outline syllabus/content requirements for membership without giving any indication how best they could be learned by novice or inexperienced academics. That is no surprise and indeed it is difficult to see how it could be otherwise since there would no agreement on what constituted the 'best'. Trying to identify pedagogical principles to promote learning in higher education could be said to be one of the important tasks, if not the most important, for the ILT itself. Certainly the Dearing Committee offered no help. Of course it could be that the presumption ran through the discussions of the Booth group that without reflection on experience little or no improvements in students' learning can come from the best designed courses or workshops. Nevertheless, it suggests a vital task for the ILT.

2 Preparing to launch

The ILT Planning Group was chaired by Professor Roger King and comprised representatives of a number of national bodies (see Appendix 2 for membership). It began its work shortly after that May meeting in 1998. Given the growing importance during 1989 and 1999 which the story will reveal of AP(E)L, it is important at this stage to put the Group's thinking and planning in the context of the level and extent of AP(E)L activities in institutions.

The survey conducted by the Learning from Experience Trust was completed by the end of 1999. It showed that 83 out of the 133 higher education institutions in England (78%) gave policies at either institutional or departmental level authorising the assessment of prior and experiential learning (AP(E)L), and claiming to have some AP(E)L activity. The survey revealed all kind of details about what institutions actually do and how they do it. But if record keeping continues as it is generally now in higher education, there is no means of knowing how many academic staff are engaged in AP(E)L activities in any one institution and therefore throughout the systems as a whole. Nor was it possible to assess the numbers of students being served by AP(E)L. About a hundred featured in the largest institution, but it ran down to handfuls in the smallest. Even the ten case studies of institutional practice did not reveal definitively those levels of participation.

What the survey does suggest for England, however, is that about half of the 133 institutions with some experience of AP(E)L ought not find it too difficult to produce procedures to enable their staff to use the AP(E)L route towards membership of the ILT. But that depends on their current experience of AP(E)L. It is one thing to assert that an institution has policies for AP(E)L either at institutional or departmental level, and that there is some activity. It is quite another thing to deduce from that that a particular institution is well enough equipped with procedures and practitioners to handle an AP(E)L route for the institution's experienced staff to seek membership of the ILT.

That then leaves the other half of the 133 institutions to acquire some expertise in AP(E)L if they are to offer a full service to their staff. In Scotland, which could not be covered in the survey, it is safe to assume that most HEIs are equipped to develop AP(E)L schemes for their own staffs. The reorganisation of post-secondary qualifications in Wales suggests that there also institutions will not find it too difficult to develop the necessary procedures for their own staff. The University of Ulster in Northern Ireland has some experience of AP(E)L so it also should not find too much difficulty in finding ways and means of serving its academics.

Nevertheless, it is obvious that most institutions will need to develop AP(E)L procedures if they do not have them already, unless, as they are free to do as indicated in the consultative documents, they choose to take one of two routes: either encourage individuals to apply direct to the ILT, or make arrangements with a neighbouring institution which is well equipped to make use of its facilities rather than trying to invent its own.

The commitment to AP(E)L continued with the King Group. It is in that context, which of course was unknown to anyone at the time, that this planning group submitted a paper for the CVCP meeting in the autumn of 1998 setting out comprehensively the purposes of the Institute, its activities, its structure, its funding, governance and implementation. Paragraph 10 of the Executive Summary read:

> Membership for existing staff would be available via a range of routes, including advanced standing and the accreditation of prior (experiential) learning.

There was another important commitment; the ILT would be established in April 1999. This put pressure on the Institute to devise and promulgate arrangements for the fast track to membership.

Then another paper was produced in October 1998 drawing together decisions which went to produce a policy paper 'Implementing the Vision' together with the results of various consultations. It confirmed that the key activities of the ILT should be:

> (a) accreditation of courses and other pathways in learning and teaching for staff, provided by higher education institutions and possibly others;

(b) collection, analysis and dissemination of existing research on teaching and learning practice in accessible formats for use within the Academic community;
(c) the development and encouragement of generic and subject based good practice in learning and teaching, including appropriate and effective application of communication and information technologies.

It set out two levels of membership:

Associateship: where the member is associated with the profession but is not a full practising member;
Member: upon completion of an accredited route for those practising the profession.

It set out two routes to membership. Again AP(E)L featured:

Route 1 – through successful completion of a new or appropriately modified institutional programme/pathway accredited by the ILT.
Route 2 – through recognition of an individual application based on AP(E)L/APL supported by the employing institution as meeting the requirements of accreditation.

All the constitutional points were rehearsed as were relations with other professional bodies. Interestingly there is reference to SEDA which acknowledges that its work overlaps with much of what the ILT is suppose to do. Just as interesting, there was no reference to UCoSDA but there is reference to The Higher Education Training Organisation (THETO). The remit for this body ran across all staff employed in higher education. Again it was claimed that there was no conflict of interest. THETO made recommendations to HEIs about coherent training programmes for all its staff. It had already endorsed ILT's approach for academic staff but it could recommend courses offered by the Institute of Personnel Management. Subsequently, it emerged that UCoSDA had become THETO.

In February 1999 another consultation document was circulated – ILT Consultation: The National Framework for Higher Education Teaching. It requested that the paper should be given the widest possible publicity within institutions and that responses by 19th March 1999 should be sent to the Director of Accreditation at the ILT who by that time was in post. Subsequently, the consultation period was extended to May.

Again the ILT circulated this as a consultation document on accreditation and membership. It got 114 responses from higher education institutions, 68 from subject associations and professional and statutory bodies, and 80 from individuals.

That paper set out a detailed framework of requirements to be met for membership under five headings: Design and Plan a Course; Teach and Support Learning in the subject; Assess students' learning achievements; Contribute to the Maintenance of Student Support systems; Evaluate and Improve the Teaching Process. There was considerable overlap with the Booth five suggested areas, some divergence but a totally different approach to membership requirements.

For each heading there was indicative content expressed as outcomes, with guidelines for the evidence required to meet each stated outcome, with a third column: guidelines for reflection. For example, this was what appeared under the heading of Design and Plan a Course:

Outcomes
1. Specify the learning outcomes of a course (module or unit of study).
2. Plan a structured programme of content and learning activities/ teaching strategies appropriate to the student group and the aims of objectives of the course.
3. Plan the separate learning activities/teaching sessions and the student work assignments associated with them.
4. Design and/or select a range of appropriate learning resources for the course.
5. Design appropriate ways of informing students of the outcomes and standards expected of them.

All that was in the first column of the table. The table then went into the second column.

Guidelines for Evidence
In showing how they meet the outcomes in column 1 applicants will be expected to provide evidence that they have:
- taken into account other courses (modules or units) in the students' programme;
- clearly specified intended learning outcomes, including the subject;
- specific and personal/transferable skills that students will be expected to acquire;
- identified students' learning needs in the context of their range of backgrounds and the academic level of the course;
- designed/selected appropriate learning strategies to meet these needs;

- planned the course so that it builds on students' prior development and achievement and links with teaching sessions, learning activities and assigned work in a way which supports the students' development and progression;
- designed/selected appropriate learning resources, both paper-based (e.g. course handbooks, textbooks, study guides and workbooks, handouts and worksheets) and electronic and identified the specific contribution each can make to teaching and learning;
- prepared effective ways of informing students of the purpose and structure of the course and of the tasks and standards expected of them.

So, putting those two columns together the document was proposing what academics and support staff would have to do to secure membership and what kinds of evidence they would have to produce to prove that they had done it.

There was a third column to the table but this was intended to give applicants some clues about how assessors would be scrutinising applications.

Guidelines for Reflection
In looking at the reflection on the evidence, an assessor will ask whether applicants have demonstrated a professional level of:
- attention to how students learn, different learning styles and approaches to learning;
- awareness of the diversity of learning needs within the student group;
- consideration of a range of teaching and learning strategies and the arguments for using/rejecting them;
- enquiry into the range of resources available locally and nationally and their merits and drawbacks;
- consideration of current research/scholarship in the subject and the impact it should have on the content and structure of the course.

A similar approach was adopted for each of the other design headings so that the document ended up with twenty-four outcomes to be met, each subdivided into the three columns of Outcomes, Guidelines for Evidence, and Guidelines for Reflection, each amounting to up to fifty different line entries.

As with previous consultative documents, there was a clear commitment to AP(E)L for individuals but now there was a detailed sketch of procedures for handling them. The Introduction: the Process, contained:

> The ILT will . . . support and assess the portfolios of those experienced staff applying through the AP(E)L route.

And

> Experienced staff applying through the AP(E)L route, will submit their portfolio and file of evidence either to their own institution if it is ILT accredited or to another ILT accredited institution/ group of institutions. The ILT will provide appropriate advice on registration for individuals who are not primarily attached to any one HE institution.

At this point it is vital to remember that membership was to be open to academic support staff as well as academics themselves. Current developments in learning provision through the internet and intranet as well as the evolution of the curriculum to try to keep in tune with contemporary changes in economic, employment and domestic life, mean it would be folly to do otherwise. Learning support in all its various guises will be increasingly important. If the ILT is to succeed in substantiating its claim to be a professional body to advance Learning and Teaching, membership must be open to all concerned with it in institutions. And for many of them, AP(E)L is likely to have a particular importance.

The paper offered guidelines for applicants whether taking Route 1 or Route 2. Evidence would need to be presented and organised according to the five areas mentioned above and there was quite detailed guidance of what a portfolio should contain. That was followed by another detailed statement about the procedure to be followed by institutions which submitted a programme for accreditation. At this stage the AP(E)L route was not referred to specifically. It was already assumed to be part of the regime.

It also contained a vital section on Continuing Professional Development. As with an increasing number of professional associations, to remain in good standing for continuing membership depends on evidence that further efforts have been made to remain up-to-date, or, as the document puts it: 'the maintenance, enhancement or extension of professional competence'.

As a consultation paper, it included some ten questions each covering some important aspect of the proposals being sketched. Two in particular applied to AP(E)L. Question 6 was:

What kinds of institutional support would experienced members of staff find useful when compiling a portfolio for ILT membership application via AP(E)L?

Question 7 followed on:

Does your institution currently provide such support for portfolio building and assessment?

It then used a twin approach in talking about the implications for individuals. It set out criteria for membership having outlined the routes which could be taken to lead to membership.

As criteria for membership it confirmed the five areas of professional activity for which evidence of achievement would be required:

- teaching and/or supporting learning in higher education;
- contribution to the design and planning of learning activities and/or programmes of study;
- provision of feedback and assessment of students' learning;
- contribution to the development of effective learning environments and student support systems;
- reflection on personal practice in teaching and learning and work to improve the teaching process.

There is an important note added to those requirements. The ILT says:

These areas will be interpreted flexibly and the ILT does not wish to constrain institutions that offer programmes with a distinctive focus on issues such as learning technologies, student centred learning workshop based learning or action research.

Throughout, one assumption was clear. That there would be two levels of membership: Associate and Member. But unlike the Booth Report, there was no indication as to the different requirements which would be laid on those two categories of applicants.

It is no surprise to find that the summary of the responses to that February document, issued in June 1999, made it absolutely clear that a twenty-four-item approach in such detail was completely unacceptable to the majority of HEIs, professional organisations and individuals. This in no way meant that support for the establishment of the ILT had dwindled. For the HEIs, 30% gave unconditional approval, 50% gave qualified approval, and 20% rejected the idea. The figures for professional organisations, statutory bodies and subject associations were: 20% gave unconditional approval, 65% gave qualified approval, and 15% rejected the proposal for an institute. Most of the individuals supported the overall aims of the ILT and accepted the need to enhance the status of teaching in higher education. Even so, all agreed that the framework of twenty-four categories set out in the consultation paper was far too inflexible, seemed overly bureaucratic, and were unnecessarily prescriptive.

Some responses from HEI's gave reasons for their rejection of the framework. It was pointed out that the proposed framework rested on two assumptions, neither of which was necessarily accepted: that the role of an HE teacher could be 'captured' in twenty-four outcome statements and that portfolio presentation and assessment was the best way of demonstrating professional competence. Further, it was noted that the framework represented a significant shift from the Booth proposals not only in substance and format but in context. Whereas the Booth suggestions were argued through giving them authoritative basis, the shift to the twenty-four outcomes was neither articulated nor justified in the February paper. Nor was its provenance indicated.

Also, there was some concern about the notion of Associate Membership. The paper saw two purposes in having an Associate Membership: (a) to provide a progression stage for those working towards full membership; (b) to provide an attainable level of achievement for various categories of support staff who assist in the learning process, but do not undertake the full range of teaching activities and responsibilities. It then asked this question: How many of the twenty-four outcomes do you think should be required for Associate Membership?

Given the rejection of the twenty-four outcomes in the suggested framework it is hardly surprising to see that the summary of conclusions contained this.

Many of the respondents felt that the proposed requirements for Associate Members would exclude a number of important groups of teachers and learning support staff who offered depth of experience in a relatively narrow range of areas of responsibility. Some of the groups which fell into this category were:

- library staff, laboratory demonstrators and C and IT staff;
- clinicians in medical and allied professions who teach clinical practice;

- visiting lecturers and part-time staff who combine teaching with professional practice;
- performing arts practitioners who teach in colleges of music and arts.

There was also disagreement with the suggestion in the paper that registration should be for a three-year period after which membership could be renewed provided that the CPD requirements had been logged. The consensus of the respondents was that is should be five years. There was anxiety too lest the relationship between CPD and good standing paid less attention than it should to subject advancement and its own particular pedagogy.

So, drawing together the overall impressions given by the responses to the February 1999 paper ILT Consultation: The National Framework for Higher Education Teaching, it was clear that the objections ran from the philosophical to the day-to-day details. They were:

- the need for a system that is not needlessly burdensome for potential members;
- the need for a system that reflects the diversity of learning environments and provides a basis for collaboration with other agencies and regulatory bodies working in this area;
- recognition of subject-based research and scholarly activity in teaching and learning;
- the need for both direct individual routes and institutional routes to membership;
- the need to include all staff who contribute to teaching and learning in whatever capacity including those in roles allied to teaching, part-time staff and postgraduates who teach;
- the need for an approach to continuing professional development that accommodates the requirements of other professional bodies.

And running through consultation discussions in institutions there was a suspicion that someone somewhere had ideas about centralisation.

Once the Institute had settled down from October 2001, the paper said that anyone wishing to join the ILT would be expected:

- either to have completed a programme of training on learning and teaching in higher education which has been accredited by the ILT in their own or another institution;

- or to produce a collection of evidence and a reflective commentary demonstrating their expertise and experience in the five areas (listed above).

It is important though at this point to refer again to the key role that AP(E)L was foreseen as having. Whether it was experienced academic staff or support staff, whether it was for individual applications via Route 2, whether it was following Route 1, at every stage there is provision for meeting membership requirements by reflecting on experience and thus producing evidence of the necessary achievements. And the vital feature of that for this story is that every university and college in the country is being invited to develop procedures to facilitate AP(E)L for its own academic and academic support staff, whether or not such facilities are available for students.

After that, everything went quiet!

3 The assessment of prior experiential learning (AP(E)L) in the UK since 1980

There is a delicious irony for anyone who had paid any attention to the development of AP(E)L in the UK over the last twenty years. Officially and publicly it has now been written into the script for the ILT and the part it is bound to play in its development. Twenty years ago the very idea was laughed out of court. Most academics rejected the idea that individuals could acquire knowledge and skill informally without being taught, which merited formal academic recognition. Slowly but surely the concept has got into the blood stream of parts of the higher and further education systems. At the latest count, as indicated in the previous chapter, there are some 83 higher education institutions which have public policies incorporating AP(E)L. How energetic they are in using the facility in practice is another matter. And now along comes the Dearing Committee with its recommendation for the ILT, followed by the Vice Chancellors enunciating that AP(E)L must be incorporated in its procedures as a possible route towards membership for experienced academics who choose to make application.

So AP(E)L has now been officially adopted by the ILT itself and, as has been recorded earlier, features in the documents it has put into the public domain. So what was rejected more or less out of hand a couple of decades ago, is going to become part of the regular mainstream activities for staff development within institutions. It means that significant numbers of experienced academics and some of their novice colleagues are going to experience at first hand for themselves what AP(E)L procedures actually involve and the demands they make on individuals. Furthermore, some are going to become responsible for devising schemes and procedures for their own institutions. It would be a nice academic game to play to identify some of those early sceptics and observe them as they go through the very procedures they held up to ridicule all those years ago.

But even more important is government's commitment to AP(E)L itself. It came in a surprising way. In December 1999 government issued a consultation document about education. There was no mention of the Foundation degree. But when the Secretary of State for Education and Employment made his speech in Woolwich in April 2000, taking the initiative in promoting the idea of an e-university, he paralleled it with announcing his intention of introducing a Foundation degree. It became the centrepiece for the further expansion of higher education to which it was committed. That rapid policy invention is an indication of the seriousness of that commitment. Even a skimpy reading of the consultation paper which the DfEE circulated about the Foundation degree makes it clear that providers of that new award are almost bound by its very purposes to deploy AP(E)L for its students. It is impossible to think of the proposed Foundation degree as a means of expanding access and increasing the numbers of students within the university system without taking into the reckoning the almost certainty that older, experienced men and women are going to be among those recruited. They will bring some knowledge and skills with them. And for them it will be vital to make sure that there is no risk whatsoever of them being asked to learn things and acquire skills which they may have acquired already either through their work or life experience in general. All the proven benefits in time and money will be of paramount importance for them. And there is the other side of the coin: shorter courses in respect of what students bring with them means a faster rate of graduation and hence saving to the public and increasingly the private purses of students.

But in some ways David Blunkett was going further than that. There was bound to be a strong symbolism in choosing Woolwich as the place to make his speech. Nearly forty years before, Anthony Crosland, the then Secretary of State, made his speech which presaged the establishment of polytechnics. Just as that was a turning point for higher education so it is as if Blunkett was wanting to put his stamp on another turning point and serving notice that he was in earnest about his two proposals.

So it turns out that while the Secretary of State has declared a further set of expectations of higher education, to wit AP(E)L, the ILT is engaged in a nationwide programme for professional staff development which fits neatly with those expectations. If there is an irony therefore about the way AP(E)L is being promulgated through the ILT, there is an entirely fortuitous coincidence between that and the needs which are implicit in the notion of a Foundation degree. What is more, as given in some detail in Chapter 2, the Secretary of State is talking in this way at a time when there are a significant number of HEIs who are well practised and experienced in offering AP(E)L to their students. Those institutions are almost bound to have introduced already various schemes for work-based learning probably for part-time degrees so that many are ready and poised to react to Blunkett's insistence that the new award should not be a shorter version of the existing proliferation of academic degrees.

The pursuit of AP(E)L began in Britain in the early 1980s with Sir Charles Carter, the Founding Vice Chancellor of Lancaster University, enabling Norman Evans to get the Policy Studies Institute (PSI) interested in the idea that there were many adults in the world outside that of formal education who were without educational qualifications but were probably well able to cope with a higher education course of study. More, there was the possibility that some had even learned enough to merit formal recognition for knowledge and skill which was the equivalent to what they might have studied in a university or college.

The American Cooperative Assessment of Experiential Learning project (CAEL) 1974–1977 was the inspiration. Funded by the Carnegie Foundation and later the Ford Foundation, the Lilley Endowment and the government agency the Fund for the Improvement of Post Secondary Education, its brief was to show that valid, reliable and affordable assessment of non-school learning was feasible. It came to be known as the assessment of prior experiential learning or PLA as its acronym. The prestigious American Testing Service at Princeton was to ensure that the research was sound. Under the leadership of Morris Keeton a coalition of universities and colleges did the field work to ensure that the results could be used in institutions. Over that three-year period some $2.1 million was contributed to the project. A whole host of research papers were published and a series of four times a year publications was issued by Jossey-Bass under the title of *New Directions in Experiential Learning*.

This meant that the early discussions could draw on a substantial body of published research based on extensive fieldwork to check out what was practicable in institutions. It had to be read cautiously because of differences between the American and British systems. Assessment regimes were different. The UK needed a set of procedures which could measure up to the requirements of Examination Boards and External Examiners. So the search was on to find the most rigorous set of procedures in the US and then work out how to adapt them for the UK. Norman Evans was able to do this through CAEL by a small director's grant from the W.K. Kellogg Foundation which enabled him to cross the USA visiting institutions which had participated in the earlier fieldwork trials.

By contrast with the funding put into the PLA developments in the USA, while grants were secured from the Further Education Unit (FEU) and the Council for National Academic Awards (CNAA), as they both were known then, in all they amounted to not much more than £20,000 to put in the ground floor for subsequent developments in AP(E)L. There was no possible body of institutional collaborators in sight. Nor were there Charities and Foundations to turn to for financial help as in the US. However, there was a small group of interested academics drawn from polytechnics, a residential college for adults and universities who believed there was something in this idea that adults could bring with them to an institution knowledge and skill which might prove academically significant. They met and speculated how to attempt to formulate ways in which the idea could be introduced to Britain.

But if by contrast with the US the grant money was puny, the differences between the two systems worked to British advantage. Here, there was a nationwide system. There, where the Federal government had little or no direct responsibility, the fifty states were directly involved, making for considerable differences between them. And while in America the Regional Accrediting Associations were charged to ensure that institutions adhered to appropriate standards, unlike the British Council for National Academic Awards they had no academic authority over the curriculum which was epitomised in the UK by CNAA's degree awarding powers. Nor was there anything comparable to the Further Education Unit.

Thus, the UK had the huge advantage over the Americans of attracting support from two national bodies, the FEU and CNAA. For both of them the starting point was to investigate the extent to which, if at all, assessments of prior experiential learning were used for admission to award bearing courses in either further or higher education. Both projects meant visiting scores of further education colleges and polytechnics. So when the result for the FEU was published as 'Curriculum opportunity, a map of experiential learning for entry to award bearing courses' – it went into three printings, 1983, 1984 and 1987 – and a copy was sent to every post-secondary education institution in the land, it was playing to a semi-prepared audience. Similarly when 'Access to higher education: non-standard entry to CNAA first degree and DipHE courses' was published by CNAA in 1984 and went to all its associated institutions, again some of the ground had been prepared through the inquiries conducted to produce the report.

Markers were put down. Notice was served for all who cared to see that AP(E)L was on the national map. But the vital thing about putting down those markers is that both the FEU and CNAA acted as national conduits of influence which between them reached into every higher and further education establishment in the land, and from the FEU to many employers. Both reports attracted significant press coverage as well.

However, it was one thing to put down markers. It was quite another to produce hard evidence of what could be done. The first opportunity came in 1982 when the Wates Foundation listened to the general idea. It then made a small grant to help launch a formally provided course called Making Experience Count. Run jointly by Goldsmiths College and what was then Thames Polytechnic, this was the first attempt in the UK to organise a formal course with the sole purpose of enabling adults to identify and formulate an account of what they had learned informally and to have it assessed. The course was for three hours a week and lasted twelve weeks. It was successful. Some of the twenty-five who enrolled on the first course in 1983 used their portfolios of evidence to advance their careers in employment. Some were enabled to apply successfully for degree studies although they did not have the formal education requirements for entry. Others realised that higher education was not for them at that time and enrolled in courses in further education colleges. Some wanted to pursue their studies but came to realise that they needed preparatory courses to get them ready for it. And some others said they had enough of learning for the time being, which was a positive reaction and just went away. Each of those 'results' from the course was a success story.

Making Experience Count went into the catalogues of both institutions and traces of its influence run through those institutions to this day. But more immediately, the course became a working demonstration of AP(E)L in practice visited by all and sundry as a rudimentary dissemination programme. Nothing like it in the country had been attempted before. So for anyone who heard of the idea of the assessment of prior experiential learning and thought about the possibilities of using it in their own institution, there was something to look at as a potential model. It was the first piece of hard evidence that there were valid and reliable ways of assessing informally acquired knowledge and skill so that it could be recognised academically. But it was only a very modest start. Even so, it attracted the attention of the Chief Inspector of further and higher education for what was then the Inner London Education Department. He could see, as could Jack Mansell, Chief Officer of the FEU, that potentially AP(E)L was a powerful instrument for the institutional change which colleges of further education were about to face. So he told his central curriculum and staff development unit to pick up what it could from MEC and try to develop similar schemes for colleges in the London area. Since the ILEA was far and away the most influential local education authority in the land, like CNAA for higher education, with the FEU, it sent a strong message to the further education world.

The next important stage of development came in 1984. CNAA funded a project to be run through the Policy Studies Institute (PSI) to 'negotiate, establish, monitor and appraise schemes for the assessment of prior experiential learning (AP(E)L) in polytechnics and colleges'. It meant doing it for real in ten of its associated institutions and as far as possible covering the entire higher education curriculum. The tally was as follows as they then were known:

City of Birmingham Polytechnic – production engineering (p/t) and business studies (p/t): now the University of Central England.
Bristol Polytechnic – business studies (p/t): now University of the West of England.
Essex Institute of Higher Education – MEd. (p/t): now Anglia Polytechnic University.
Newcastle upon Tyne Polytechnic – associate degree scheme: now Northumbria University.
Polytechnic of North London – evening degree (p/t): now University of North London.
Sheffield City Polytechnic – social studies (p/t) and business studies (p/t): now Sheffield Hallam University.
Stockport College of Technology – mechanical engineering (p/t).
The Polytechnic, Wolverhampton – computing and information technology – (p/t and f/t): now Wolverhampton University.
Middlesex Polytechnic – modular degree scheme – (p/t and f/t): now Middlesex University.
Thames Polytechnic – continuing education: now Greenwich University.

That two-and-half-year project resulted in CNAA's Development Service publication No. 17 in 1987: *Assessing Prior Experiential Learning*. It served as a handbook for those institutions thinking about introducing AP(E)L schemes. Most of the problems and issues which have arisen since about AP(E)L got a preliminary outing in that publication: the preparation of learning claims; tutorial roles; assessment; student guidance; the difference between disciplines; staff development – it was all there. Equally important, given CNAA's academic role nationally and its standing, it set the national seal of academic authority on any institution wishing to develop schemes of their own. Additionally, those ten institutions were dotted around the country so that as well as a spread of disciplines there was a geographical distribution as well.

That project overlapped with two other important developments: one by CNAA as a national body, and the other by the establishment of the Learning from Experience Trust as a small educational charity which set out to act as a ginger group to promote AP(E)L as best it could. AP(E)L was helped along from two directions during the mid-1980s and onwards. May 1986 was the key date. It saw the introduction by CNAA of its Credit Accumulation and Transfer Registry; the first time in this country that facilities provided for credit accumulation to run across institutions and not merely within institutions as had been the discussion point up to then. That CNAA initiative stimulated two related additional ways of organising the academic work of universities, polytechnics as they then were, and some colleges and institutes of higher education. A credit accumulation system meant organising academic courses on a term, semester or half-year basis instead of conceiving them as programmes of continuous study for a whole year. This simplified the possible introduction of an AP(E)L strand of activity for the obvious reason that is was much more likely that the informally acquired knowledge and skill of an individual could be related to a shorter rather than a longer course.

One of the arguments for introducing credit accumulation schemes was that it extended student choice. Not being committed to linear courses which locked them into one or more disciplines for the entirety of their three years of study, the theory was that credit accumulation would enable students to some extent to build their academic programme in ways which they decided rather than having it all decided for them almost at admission. But for wider choice to mean anything, students needed more information on what to base decisions about the various courses they might be considering. One way of coping with that was to extend the syllabus descriptions of the shorter courses by adding learning outcomes to them. This was the second influence on academic organisation prompted by the CATS Registry at CNAA. This was in no way an academic version of behavioural objectives. It was simply a set of statements about what it was intended to offer students as learning opportunities and what it was hoped that they would be able to do and know at the end of the course.

Just as credit accumulation made it easier to see how, organisationally, an institution could introduce AP(E)L facilities, so learning outcomes, or intentions as it is perhaps more appropriate to call them, made it easier to see how academics could accommodate AP(E)L. Right from the beginning it was clear that what was learned from experience needed to be expressed in terms which fitted academic study, that any claim to possess certain knowledge and skill had to be supported directly by evidence and that the evidence had to be acceptable to an academic assessor. It was obvious that a combination of syllabus description and learning intentions could become an assessment tool for academics considering learning claims based on informally acquired learning. It was also obvious that students could make more informed decisions about the courses that they chose to enrol on if they too were equipped with that information.

But the CNAA CATS Registry did more than that. When all the sometimes contentious negotiations were over CNAA's Council took the decision to establish the CATS Registry. That meant writing regulations for the operation of a facility in higher education which had not existed before in the UK. If credit accumulation was to mean anything in practice for students, the shorter courses within any CATS scheme had to be credit rated against credit requirements for the completion of a certificate after one year, a diploma after two years and a degree after three years of study. It was decided to set each of three years at 120 credits, making 120, 240 for the certificate and diploma respectively, with 360 required for the completion of a degree. With some variations that tariff has served as a template for CATS systems wherever institutions have developed such a scheme.

The CATS Registry did two other things, both of which supported the promulgation of the AP(E)L concept. The CATS Registry rule book wrote in that academic credit awarded through AP(E)L was countable towards a higher education award at both undergraduate and post-graduation levels. Immediately that gave AP(E)L a currency which was different in kind from the small-scale work which preceded it. Once that book of regulations was made public, any institution associated with CNAA was free to introduce schemes of its own. And some did so quickly, notably as front runners what was then Middlesex Polytechnic, Thames Polytechnic, Wolverhampton Polytechnic and the City of Sheffield Polytechnic.

The regulations went further than that. The planning group saw CNAA's CATS as an opportunity for achieving a closer and different form of collaboration between higher education, the professions and the world of industry and business. It took note of the large number of courses offered by professional associations to their members and the growing number of education and training courses offered by employers to their employees. Taking its cue from the overall reasoning behind the assessment of prior and experiential learning, it decided that to exploit the possibilities offered by the CATS Registry it needed a formula for credit rating such of those courses as could be demonstrated to meet the requirements of a higher education course. It was decided that four credits represented the smallest amount of study which could justify inclusion as higher education study. That worked out as the equivalent of one week's full-time study.

It is not to much to say that the face of higher education was changed irrevocably by the combination of the recognition of academic credit for AP(E)L at both undergraduate and postgraduate levels and the facility for including as higher education study in-house courses offered by employers or professions. Some of the polytechnics were quick to use these regulations as a means of developing new forms of collaboration with local employers. Some national companies went direct to CNAA and some stayed with their local polytechnic. But the scene was set for further developments down the AP(E)L track and what came to be called work-based learning.

All this overlapped with the establishment of the Learning from Experience Trust in 1986, following six years of preparatory work at the PSI. It saw itself and still does as a ginger group to promote the ideas implicit in AP(E)L in all ways possible. The Trust assumed responsibility for the CNAA project with the ten institutions. Almost simultaneously, the introduction of CNAA's CATS Registry opened the way for the Trust to pioneer two other vital developments in trying to capture for academic assessment learning acquired outside formal education institutions. One was the first effort to put an academic value on in-house courses provided by employers. The other was the first essay into what has come to be called Work-Based Learning (WBL). Both were not more than piloting in practice the opportunities written into the CATS regulations.

The first was the Validation of Companies' In-House Courses. The idea was to run an academic slide rule over courses provided by major employers for their employees, and if they came up to academic requirements for higher education, to put a value ticket on them citing the amount of academic credit recommended and its level. The credit accumulation facilities then available through the CATS Registry and through those institutions which developed their own internal arrangements enabled anyone who had completed satisfactorily the course under question to be awarded that credit towards a higher education award.

This offered new and additional ways of thinking about collaboration between the world of work and that of higher education. The investment by employers into the education and training of their own employees for their own purposes could, where suitable, be exploited in ways which benefited both them and their employees. Government in the shape of the Department of Employment had woken up to the possibilities offered by the CATS Registry which is why it funded for Trust to undertake this project. Sainsbury's, ICL, Wimpey Foods, as then it was, joined in this project. One of the byproducts of this project was a sometimes fractious argument about assessment. As employers sat down with academics to consider which if any courses they wished to put forward for consideration as a credit rating, they had to recognise that they were bound to be unacceptable unless they had a stringent assessment system to determine what it was that their employees had learned as opposed to being present. This became a two-way traffic. Employers saw the advantages for themselves of tightening up their own arrangements. Academics learned a good deal about the realities of the working world which got translated into curricula revisions. As so often is the case, something which starts out to do one thing, ends up with doing something additional if not different. It was the CATS Registry and its rule book which alone made this possible. It was AP(E)L for academics and employers by another name.

At the same time the Department of Employment funded the Trust to develop as a pilot project the idea of Learning Agreements for Employees. Based on the proposition that men and women can and often do learn from what they do in their day-to-day work the scheme was to devise a learning programme for each individual participant which comprised what it was an individual wanted to learn, material which the employer would find it valuable for the employees to master, all in ways which met the requirements of an academic supervisor. Each individual learning agreement had three parts: a statement of what was to be learned; an account of how it was to be learned and, most important, how the learning was to be assessed academically to determine the amount and level of credit to be awarded when it was completed. Employee, employer and academic signed off on the learning agreements which served as official documents for monitoring progress. One vital factor which contributed to the success of the work was that learning agreements could be renegotiated. The importance of that was that whether full time or part time, up until that time most formally provided courses did not allow for interruptions to the study schedule if work commitments or domestic arrangements made it impossible to follow a course as intended. The built-in possibility for re-negotiation of agreed working schedule in the Learning for Employees project changed all that. It introduced a flexibility which had hardly existed before. It meant that if the agreed learning schedule could not be adhered to, there was nothing to prevent a rescheduling for the convenience of the learner.

Six volunteers were recruited from each of four employers: at its own insistence a government department, the Manpower Services Commission of the Department of Employment; Jaguar, the high prestige car manufacturer; a computer company, JBS Computers; and Wimpey, the restaurant chain. Each was linked with a polytechnic which provided an academic supervisor for its associated six volunteers; Sheffield, Coventry, Wolverhampton and Oxford respectively. Most of the twenty-four took their studies further, some gained credit for their learning agreement at Master's level, and some gained promotion as a result of the learning achievements they had accomplished.

It turned out of course that some of the employees could claim academic credit for the in-house courses they had completed where they had been validated academically. Others made claims against the prior experiential learning they had acquired. In effect therefore it meant that both employees and employers were sitting on three sources of potential academic credit and they did not know it. The project established an additional route towards graduation. This brought AP(E)L into a different context. Not merely was it showing the way for closer collaboration between employers and higher education; it was related to schemes for widening participation and expanding access. Another byproduct of this project was that by adding Oxford and Coventry to the ten participating institutions in the previous CNAA project, the geographical coverage was extended of institutions which had significant experience of working with AP(E)L.

The Department of Employment was impressed. Thus it became the third national conduit for promoting these ideas within higher education through its ability to fund initiatives which looked as if they would further government policies of widening access and of beginning to meet the early anxiety of increasing the employability of recently qualified graduates. Its initial scepticism turned into enthusiastic support and from 1987/8 for the next ten years or so it spent millions annually on funding variations of both those initial experiments with Work-Based Learning in an expanding number of institutions. The general proposition was established that significant learning can be acquired without necessarily having contact with formal institutions.

The question was the extent to which that proposition was understood, accepted and seen as a reference point for future action. The survey conducted by the Trust of AP(E)L activities tells part of the story. As reported earlier, there are eighty-three HEIs which say that either at institutional or departmental level they have policies for the implementation of AP(E)L. So far there is no authoritative account of the range and nature of Work-Based Learning (WBL) activities. Put the two together, however, and it is a reasonable guess that about half of the institutions in the system are currently practising some form of AP(E)L or WBL or a combination of both.

During the late 1980s the Department of Employment funded the Trust to undertake another two projects which were trying to carry AP(E)L to areas which at that time were untouched. The first was the potential of AP(E)L in universities. The Universities of Kent at Canterbury, Warwick and Nottingham with Goldsmiths College as a fourth participated. This time the investigation concerned the extent to which universities could see benefit in the general idea and then to introduce some schemes of implementation. A report under that name was published by the Trust and like its predecessors went to every higher and further education institution in the land.

The second was perhaps one of the most exciting projects the Trust undertook during that period: Work-Based Learning for Academic Credit. AP(E)L ran through it from start to finish. Chester College, John Moores Liverpool University and Liverpool University were the partners with the Trust. Despite its title, the project was nothing to do with what regular employees learned from their work. The Trust had pioneered that some years before. Nor did it relate closely to sandwich courses which incorporated periods of work experience. This was a different form of pioneering. It was concerned with curriculum development for full-time undergraduates. The idea was to take full-time undergraduates studying non-vocational degrees out of their classroom and laboratories for one whole term, making one-ninth of their course, so that they could spend four days a week with an employer and have one day a week back in the institution for de-briefing and follow small-scale courses about the economy and the place of firms in it. The learning they acquired would then count for the same amount of academic credit as if they were still sitting in their classrooms. And one critical aspect of the project was that it concerned students on non-vocational degrees and not those on courses which included a work experience as preparation for professional occupations.

This was something of a different order from work experience. It was AP(E)L at work at several different levels. For a start, the three very different institutions had to work out a common learning plan; what it was reasonable to expect students might be able to learn, and find a common set of learning intentions which could apply to all students whatever type of firm, business or other employing body they found themselves in. Moreover, the three institutions then had to agree a common marking scheme. A learning agreement was negotiated between employer, student and the institutions' supervisor which in standard form indicated what was to be learned, how it was to be learned, what evidence could be adduced, and how it was to be assessed.

This amounted to a planned programme for full-time students to acquire experiential learning and then have it assessed as part of their regular undergraduate studies. As such, for the academics involved it was a fairly thoroughgoing programme of staff development about the ins and outs of AP(E)L, as tutors from the three participating institutions tried to find common positions on quite unfamiliar ground. For the students it was a huge success as an element of curriculum development. They found it stimulating, a welcome addition to formal studies, giving them social and economic context in which to place their studies. In addition to the overall maturing which could be predicted, tutors remarked on the improved application students showed in their classroom study as a result of seeing what they were learning in that wider context which work with employers had given them. The employers asked for more. And the institutions proceeded to integrate the scheme into their regular course provision.

Meantime the FEU maintained its interest of AP(E)L. It funded the Trust to conduct a survey of assessment schemes and later to consider the role of guidance as part of Student Services in further education colleges as well as funding individual colleges to develop one scheme or another. But increasingly from 1986 when the National Council for Vocational Qualifications (NCVQ) was established, NVQs became a different preoccupation. Because each National Vocational Qualification and its component units was designed to facilitate assessment only without any reference to the source of the skill and knowledge which was required for each unit and NVQ, it was committed to AP(E)L from its very first day. But with a difference. Whereas for NCVQ assessment it was on a pass or fail basis, so that was the limit to its use of AP(E)L; for higher education it had had a whole range of uses beyond assessment. It spoke to admissions, pedagogy, curricula development and student support services. Some in HEIs saw it as an educational programme in its own right. So while under the impact of the NCVQ further education colleges were forced into taking note of AP(E)L, they were not able to use it to act as an institutional catalyst for change as it could, and in many cases did, in universities and colleges of higher education. Moreover, despite the somewhat heady rhetoric about rating Level 4 NVQs as equivalent to undergraduate study and Level 5 to postgraduate study, and despite the willingness of some universities and colleges to find ways of integrating NVQs with their regular course provision, it seems fair to say that NCVQ had little impact on higher education. And to that extent the wider purposes of AP(E)L were pursued by those institutions which wished to do so.

And they did, for during the 1990s AP(E)L developments in higher education quickened their pace. This was largely due to the efforts of the Department of Employment (DE) and then the amalgamated Department for Education and Employment (DfEE) to urge, stimulate, cajole and persuade universities in general to pay more attention to the employability of their newly qualified graduates as this became a more prominent element in government policies. Hence the DE and then the DfEE put out a succession of project specifications to tender, where employability was the prime consideration. So inevitably the majority of projects, scores of them, were concerned one way or another with WBL. And there can be no WBL without some form of AP(E)L.

Meantime, from the mid-1980s onwards there was a staff development programme to promote AP(E)L in both higher and further education. This was no officially organised effort. Through the good offices of an American body known then as the Council for the Advancement of Experiential Learning, the W.K. Kellogg Foundation funded a limited programme under the title of the Scholar Exchange Programme. The idea was to identify institutional leaders, those with an influence on public policy, and middle ranging institutional staff with their hands on levers to make things happen, and take them to the USA to see for themselves how American colleges and universities made use of AP(E)L. This began during the PSI stage of development and then became a prime activity of the Learning from Experience Trust.

It was a highly selective programme by invitation or recommendation only. Whether invited or recommended, participants came only from those institutions where it was clear that some subsequent action was a high probability. The basis for the programme was a group of four people from different institutions, spending a week together with the Director of the Trust who knew the American institutions very well, visiting some six or seven community colleges and four-year colleges and universities up and down the East Coast from Boston to Washington, with a no-holds-barred brief to probe as deeply and as sceptically as they could. Their hosts knew what they were in for and welcomed the awkward questions and sometimes scepticism which the visitors brought with them. They said it made them think harder about what they were doing.

By seeing to it that participants came from different parts of the country so that there was some kind of geographical coverage, the Study Tours – as they were called – amounted to a rudimentary dissemination programme. This was particularly effective when it was possible to link Study Tour participation to senior staff from the ten participating institutions in the CNAA project mentioned earlier. Indeed so successful were the Study Tours that instead of being limited to the twenty members which the Kellogg funding had specified, by 1994 some 160 senior British academics and administrators had had that experience of AP(E)L. It became a self-financing operation. An evaluation was conducted of the Study Tours and published with the title of *Learners All – Worldwide*. The programme is referred to in greater detail in Chapter 9.

This then was the context and level of understanding of the theory and practice of AP(E)L by the time the Dearing Committee reported in July 1997. And hence it was the context in which the CVCP's Booth planning group did its work in response to the Dearing recommendation for the establishment for the Institute of Learning and Teaching.

Now in 2000 it all seems very familiar to many, even old hat. That is the measure of the distance travelled by AP(E)L in twenty years. With nearly 50% of the HEIs signed up one way or another, that is what the ILT is inheriting.

4 Coming to terms with AP(E)L: institutions and individuals

AP(E)L has featured prominently in the evolution of the ILT right from the beginning of the Booth group's consultations through to the publication by the ILT of its regulations for both institutional accreditation and individual membership. This means that many institutions which have given no thought to ways of certificating uncertificated knowledge and skill for students now are likely to have to take note of it for the benefit of their own academic staff. And for many this is not easy either for the institution or its academic staff.

Some find some difficulty in coming to terms with the theory as well as the practice of AP(E)L. The theory asserts that the acquisition of learning is not necessarily confined to formal academic institutions, and that currently we live in a world where learning can take place anywhere: in work, in leisure and in just living. The practice asserts that such learning can be assessed validly and reliably, as meriting formal academic recognition at higher education levels, if it meets the necessary requirements.

It is hardly surprising that both the theory and practice of AP(E)L are not only unfamiliar but unwelcome for many academics steeped in their disciplines, conscious of the expectations for research results which they now have to cope with, whatever priorities they gave to teaching, research and their own lives in the past. They have quite enough change to cope with during the past twenty years: more students, with lower units of resource for each, which inevitably means higher staff/student ratios. Accountability, transparency, and standards sweep through official paper after paper with what appears to be an insatiable appetite for ever more detail. This seems to many to be based on the misapprehension that the more that is put on paper the greater the transparency and hence enhanced accountability. There is a surprising naivety about some of these efforts. The Higher Education Quality Council, which most thought was modestly helpful to institutions, gave way to the

Quality Assurance Agency (QAA), which many consider to be badly mistaken in its attempts to design a single standards template with benchmarks and codicils galore to fit what is acknowledged to be a considerably diverse system within the mass higher education the country now has. Every one of the QAA's initiatives seem to make more demands upon individual academics. So too do the unending series of circulars and demand notes from the Funding Council. Add in the Research Assessment Exercise which affects every tutor in the system with an eye on career implications while it can affect an institution's funding levels. Government then presses the cause of employability as if higher education had ignored it in the past. None of this means that academics and their institutions are denying the need for being more open about what they do and how they do it and to try to keep the curriculum in tune with the changes in contemporary society so that the public can be reassured that its tax money is being well spent. There are just too many demands for too much of the time. There is little doubt that for the majority of academics they are seriously overpressed and overstretched.

Now along comes the Institute of Learning and Teaching. Like the RAE it impinges on both individuals and their institution. Individuals have their futures to think about. Institutions have to be ready for their funding forms to contain in the future little boxes showing the number and proportion of their academic and support staff who are members of the ILT with money docked or added accordingly. More pressure then on both individuals and institutions. And if all that is not enough, now there are both the role and operating implications for institutions and their academic staff of the inclusion of AP(E)L in the rules and regulations of the ILT.

In trying to come to terms with it, right at the beginning it is vital to differentiate between prior and experiential. The parenthesis is the clue. Both tend to get lumped together in discussions about AP(E)L causing unnecessary confusion. Prior is fairly straightforward. It is fairly easy to accept that the results of successfully completed formal education courses taken in other places and for other purposes may, provided they meet the requisite academic requirements, count either for admission or for some form of advanced standing. That is prior learning. For example, when a student moves from the first year in one institution and goes directly into the second year of another institution, the academic credits gained in the first institution and accepted by the new receiving institution is prior learning. So is the 'Higher' National Diploma. Almost automatically an applicant to read an engineering or business studies degree who has completed successfully an HND will be awarded 120 credits which on a credit accumulation system puts that applicant in the second year, always assuming that the course content of what has been studied is acceptable as the foundation for the new studies. That is a decision for the receiving institution. At admission level there is a range of public and professional qualifications which can stand in lieu of standard entry requirements.

Experiential learning is also prior, but refers to learning which has been acquired without reference to formal education provision. This is all of a piece with the recognition that there are so many opportunities for learning nowadays which are open to individuals. Natural history, the environment – local, national and international – archeology, history, literature and fine art; any cursory skimming of the week or so's programmes on the television shows the vast array of possibilities for individuals to learn in ways which only thirty years ago would have required books and lectures. The internet is a very sophisticated extension of TV as a learning facility. And of course it plays directly to those for whom learning visually is a powerful complement to trying to learn from text on the page. Similarly, a glance at the vast array of specialist magazines on the shelves of a newsagent indicate the large numbers of people who want to pursue their interests, often at quite sophisticated levels. Then there is personal study through reading, and as a declining activity, attending classes which are not credit and award bearing.

There is of course Work-Based Learning (WBL). It is now axiomatic that unless employees continue to learn, their employer can be at risk. Continued learning within a company means survival. Without it bankruptcy can threaten. Now not all that 'survival learning' is so company specific that it does not lie within the higher education requirements for learning. And given the huge pressure for companies to develop themselves as places of learning, this represents another body of people whose experiential learning, what they have learned from their work, may well merit the award of academic credits.

During the past ten years or so the Department for Education and Employment has put increasing pressure on universities and colleges through its grant awarding priorities, to develop various schemes for WBL as part of the overall thrust to try and enhance the employability of graduating students. There is no sign that this pressure will decrease. What is more, the expansion of student numbers is due for another boost from government, and many of those who can be pursuaded to apply to use the system will be relatively untutored and therefore AP(E)L candidates. It is difficult not to see how in those circumstances an increasing number of institutions will find themselves needing to provide services for candidates without the formal entry requirements. In the context of 'Coming to terms with AP(E)L' this could be of vital importance. It means that academics are likely to be making academic judgements about claims to learning over which neither they nor their institution may have had much influence despite the fact that WBL may be integral to the institution's formal provision of courses.

The sum total of all this is that there are people without the formal education qualifications required for entry to higher education who have acquired knowledge and skill which makes them well able to cope with a degree course of study. More than that, there are significant numbers of those people who can prove they have sufficient knowledge to merit being awarded academic credit towards a degree.

Experiential learning is far harder than prior learning for some experienced academics to accept let alone get enthusiastic about. However, time and again it has proved to be the case that hardened sceptics can change their views of experiential learning when they have found themselves assessing submissions for academic credit. Oftentimes they are astonished at the breadth and depth of the understanding which an untutored man or woman can show. It is also clear from the experience of the last twenty years, that academic staff who have had some experience of working in the manufacturing, commercial or business world find it an easier proposition to accept. This is because they know from their own experience that what they learned from their work was of vital importance for their performance at work, and when they think about it sometimes more important than what they learned for their degrees.

But for others, sometimes there is an unfortunate double twist to the argument against accepting AP(E)L. If, so goes this line of thought, AP(E)L is going to result in students being given credit for some of the modules in a particular discipline, logically it means that they will not be in classes offered by that discipline and therefore the discipline will lose money, run the risk of reducing further staffing levels and raising all manner of complicated questions about quality. And further, here comes the second twist: it also follows logically from credit being given to students for modules of study where they have not attended any classes given for that module, that for some an uncomfortable and nagging uncertainty enters an academic's life. Ghastly thought. Does this mean that I am unnecessary – redundant?

The response to both of these objections to AP(E)L – and they are the same as some of those raised right round the world – is 'not so'. First, experience shows that the awarding of credit towards higher education awards acts as a powerful recruiting agency. Students who would not otherwise consider approaching a formal education institution can appear in enrolment lists. In other words an institution proclaiming its commitment to AP(E)L is likely to enrol students who would otherwise not be there. It can mean that more students rather then fewer are on the books. This is because a university or college which has reference in its prospectus or course catalogue to the possibilities for academic credit derived from prior experiential learning is sending a different message from those which do not. In effect, it is inviting people to bring with them whatever learning they have acquired, no matter where from, and the college or university will say what it is worth academically in terms of the awards the institution offers and how it might be used as a basis for further learning.

To begin with, the second objection is psychological. For those academics who feel that way, AP(E)L is threatening. Probably it is the experience of reading some AP(E)L claims with its supporting evidence alone that will change their view. It can be because of perfectly proper anxieties about academic standards. Enormous amounts of time are now spent on quality assurance. Naturally there will be hostility for anything which looks as if it might compromise the systems for quality which have been build up with such care. One way to meet this anxiety is to note that different assessment procedures can be used for different disciplines. Mathematicians may see tests as the best way of eliciting what skills and knowledge a candidate may have acquired already; whereas a more discursive approach supplemented with an interview may be the best way of assessing the level and extent of learning of a candidate offering, say, business management or social sciences. But the crunch argument in meeting this anxiety about quality is to remind academics that they themselves are the assessors and so quality rests in their own hands.

There is yet another way of looking at the question for those who are prepared to think about it. Assessing learning which has been acquired without reference to the tutor doing the assessing or to the institution where the tutor teaches, is by definition extending the role of that academic. The judgement used to make assessments of work produced by students attending the institution is being applied on a wider scale, extending academic authority rather than diminishing it. So instead of becoming less necessary, academics can become more necessary but in a different way from heretofore. Roles not only change, but enlarge. At a time when the world is awash with demands for higher education to become more responsive to the world which supports it, this can be a powerful argument and demonstration of increased responsiveness through evidence of activity on the ground.

Intellectual arguments aside, there are significant organisation and procedural issues to be faced by any institution which seeks to implement policies for AP(E)L. The first concerns the way the academic work of the institutions is organised and administered; some form of credit accumulation. The obvious point is that awarding credit for AP(E)L is more readily facilitated where courses are shorter rather than longer. For example, it is extremely unlikely that an adult enthusiast for history would have covered in his/her reading the content of a year-long programme on, say, nineteenth-century constitutional and legal reform affecting central and local government. But such an enthusiast might well know a great deal about the shenanigans surrounding the 1832 and 1867 acts. By extension, if there are some open box modules or space for options in the credit accumulation system then the scope for awarding AP(E)L credit widens. It does not then have to be related specifically to courses in the prospectus. Eclectic learning can be expressed in terms which faciliate reliable and valid assessment like any other form of learning. Eclectic learning, whatever it is called, can therefore feature for assessment.

Many academics resist the very idea of credit accumulation, often through a misapprehension of its implications. The most common is the presumption that modularisation leads inexorably to cafeteria style degrees so that the sanctity of subjects is threatened, an argument which can appear to be more in the tutor's interest than concerns about students' learning. However, there are two vital points about credit accumulation which touch on AP(E)L. It does not follow that specialised study of disciplines is inhibited. In that history example, all it need mean is that the former year-long course can become a succession of shorter courses. It does mean, however, that some students are enabled to take some but not all those courses in nineteenth century history. The range of student choice is extended. Student numbers could even increase. How far this choice extends depends on whether the credit accumulation runs across the entire institution or whether it is limited to particular areas of study in departments or faculties.

There is another aspect to credit accumulation which causes resentment and often scepticism among some academics but is of fundamental importance for the satisfactory operation of AP(E)L: learning outcomes. For some there is something almost commonsensical about writing down against a syllabus what is to be studied, an outline of what it is assumed that students will have learned by the end of the course. If that is not clear in the mind of a tutor it is extremely likely that students will have only hazy ideas of what they are supposed to grasp, so goes that argument. Contrarily some academics consider the writing of learning outcomes as a piece of intrusive bureaucracy which is more to do with regulation than with student learning. This argument goes further. It claims that the validity of learning outcomes is based on a false premise. It appears to presuppose that what students will learn from any course is what the tutor intends that they shall learn. Anyone who has any experience of teaching knows that that is not the case. What students learn from a tutor is a highly idiosyncratic business. No matter what a tutor tries to teach, students will take from the teaching what they take. And that is entirely unpredictable. Indeed, such a position is the very basis of education anywhere. Learning is unpredictable. But that does not say that tutors and their institutions need not do their best to help students along the learning path. Learning outcomes can assist in that way. Learning intentions is perhaps a better way of expressing it. Intentions can either be realised or not realised. The mechanistic flavour of outcomes is avoided.

An additional reason for resentment derives from the marking load which results from a larger number of shorter courses than the fewer longer courses which used to be the norm. And it is true that in many cases the load has become nearly intolerable. In some ways, however, that is because the marking procedures which were commonly used for the longer courses which used to exist have been transferred lock, stock and barrel to the shorter courses. There is something nonsensical about that. It was understandable that to begin with, confronted with the requirements of quality assurance, the same battery of measures were used to mark students' work from the shorter courses. But in all probability it has been taken too far. And even here AP(E)L may have something to offer. Armed with learning outcomes or learning intentions tutors assessing prior experiential learning have found that experienced assessors acting as generalists can produce results which are broadly the same as those produced by subject experts. This can only be done of course where AP(E)L systems are very firmly established which probably include some version of an assessment board through which generalists and specialists have worked together and arrived at a shared confidence in the assessment procedures they follow. The lesson from that could be that adopting an over-refined detailed AP(E)L assessment regime for shorter courses may not be necessary to produce reliable and valid assessments.

But assessment redounds on students as well as academics. The complaint is often heard from academics that students do not seem to be interested in learning; they are preoccupied with passing the course. And there can be little doubt that subjecting learning to too frequent forms of official assessment is bound to strengthen that view. Anything to counteract it without damaging standards would seem worth considering. But the entire debate about learning outcomes depends on how they are written. There is no doubt that the NCVQ gave learning outcomes a bad name in higher education, with their hierarchy of competences which presumed to describe every level of performance. However, it is possible to write learning outcomes for a drama or fine art course which are framed in sufficiently broad terms to make it clear what the learning intentions are without going into prescriptive detail. And that goes for every discipline in the book.

There is a further point about learning outcomes. Within a credit accumulation system it is vital to provide students with the information they need to decide what courses they wish to follow. Being able to study the learning outcomes for different courses is for students a form of self-propelled guidance since they can look up details of courses in the library and increasingly on the internet.

Now this is important in the context of the ILT and AP(E)L for two reasons. Whatever the institutional arrangements for enabling academics to seek membership of the ILT, there is no doubt that some of the evidence of professional effectiveness will depend on tutors' familiarity with learning outcomes. Like it or not, nowadays learning outcomes are taken for granted. And not merely within institutions. Successful collaboration with professional bodies and employers can depend on all parties being crystal clear about the point of any programmes of study whether they are taken from the institution's current catalogue or are negotiated on the tailor-made basis. The second reason is that AP(E)L is about assessment. And assessment too features prominently in the ILT requirements for membership. The connection between short courses, learning outcomes and assessment makes this a critical area. It is also worth remembering that in many people's eyes AP(E)L in Britain has now reached the stage when it is increasingly unhelpful to talk about it as if were something atypical and additional to higher education practice. It is just an additional technique of assessment along with the battery of other methods used. It is the mirror image to the proposition that learning can now stem from a wide variety of sources. Just as opportunities for learning have expanded so have the assessment procedures for examining it.

What these two points illustrate is that neither constitutes a compelling argument for resisting the introduction of AP(E)L. There may be other reasons for rejecting the introduction of credit accumulation but it is a red herring to tie those objections to AP(E)L.

If that is to do with the way in which the academic affairs of an institution are organised procedurally things can be more complicated. Where assessing prior and experiential learning is a new departure for an institution, the initial decision is whether to centralise procedures or whether they should be devolved to departments or faculties or schools. The experience of the last twenty years has shown that to begin with it is wise to create a central unit to cope with all the procedural questions up to the point where academic judgements are made. Inquiries, advice on how to prepare learning claims with supporting evidence, guidance as to in which disciplines learning claims might best be made, all can be handled consistently and reliably through a designated central office. Information sheets for both staff and students need to be written in the name of the institution and which are accurate and accessible. Although it sounds simple enough, composing those information sheets can be a very tricky business. Consistency is vital in this litigious age for obvious reasons. But a central office with a clear brief can acquire experience and expertise in AP(E)L matters which later can inform whatever devolved arrangements may be introduced. Conversely, the risk is that if several different hands in several different departments undertake the initial stages there will be inconsistencies leading to untold trouble.

If a central unit is the preferred way of coping with the initial introduction of AP(E)L, it is valuable in ensuring consistency across assessment and quality assurance. It is essential that it devises ways of ensuring that it is academics in the relevant discipline who make decisions about any academic credit to be awarded. As with any regular course there needs to be an academic body/committee representative of the entire disciplinary range of the institution complete with external examiner with the responsibility of scrutinising results and authorising their entries on student records. Working as a group those academics are likely to produce criteria for assessment. By extension that will help ensure that quality assurance measures are applied to AP(E)L academic results as for the rest of the institution.

However, it needs a tough-minded institution to establish from scratch a centralised system. Inevitably there is tension between departments and a centralised set of procedures whether it is to do with finance, staff numbers, room allocation, threats of top slicing or the overall budget. A centralised AP(E)L unit has to run the same gammut of objections. What it does though is to highlight the difficulties those tensions can cause in any proposal for institutional change.

The arrival of Work-Based Learning as a growing element in the higher education curriculum makes this even more important. Because its provision is often part of regular degree programmes, it is obvious that heads of departments and their colleagues are going to be closely involved in every aspect of WBL, often on a day-to-day basis which is involvement of a different order from being asked to assess AP(E)L submissions. Unless there is a central unit with a brief to oversee and monitor procedures on an institution-wide basis and so be in a position to evaluate performance for the institution and is answerable to the academic committee referred to, there is likely to be an organisational academic nightmare.

In the fullness of time if the decision comes to devolve responsibility for AP(E)L procedures then precedents will have been set, case law accumulated, expertise developed and confidence established to deal with all the implications of AP(E)L. The danger is, and again experience demonstrates this, that sometimes devolution can lead to diminished activity. Although devolution might have been sought by departments anxious to be in charge of their own affairs, objecting to centralisation, it can easily become a chore, losing whatever momentum may have been established centrally.

Assuming that potential applicants have been given sound advice, guidance and support at earlier stages, assessment and quality assurance procedures are the obvious key to the satisfactory academic operation of an AP(E)L scheme. Understandably assessing experiential learning makes some academics nervous until they get experienced at it. Assessing a claim for knowledge and skill and considering its supporting evidence is a very different thing from assessing the work of students who have been sitting in classes or laboratories, many if not all of them known by name.

But despite the difference in origin of the learning there should be no difference in the approach to assessments. AP(E)L candidates need to be assessed as if they were sitting alongside other students in a class. In other words if 40% is the pass mark then that applies to AP(E)L assessments just like everyone else. That is a very important principle. Quite unconsciously, a concern for sustaining standards can result in tutors being more stringent in their assessment of AP(E)L scripts than classroom based scripts. That is illegitimate.

It is related to another issue – covering the ground. If a tutor is trying to assess a piece of work submitted through the AP(E)L route and is comparing it with the content of the syllabus it is easy to make judgements on the basis of the extent to which the content of the syllabus is covered. But often that is not the basis for assessing the work of students sitting in classrooms. There needs to be consistency on the part of the tutor here as with overall final grades. Another aspect of a learning claim can also be neglected; that is the conceptual understanding of the topics outlined in the course as demonstrated in the claim. This is an aspect of assessment which does not necessarily depend on covering the ground. It is where the judgement of the academic concerned comes into the reckoning.

Nowhere is this more evident than when an AP(E)L candidate submits for assessment material which relates to a subject or discipline which is not offered by the institution in its regular course provision. For the sake of the argument there is no doubt that the level of conceptual understanding displayed merits recognition at higher education level. So the institution can respond either by saying that it is unable to make an assessment of that learning because it does not teach the subject or it can react by saying that it will make arrangements to have the work assessed by someone with the necessary expertise who is outside the institution. This question raises many others, but it illustrates how AP(E)L can introduce unexpected issues.

AP(E)L assessment results have to be placed alongside all other examination results which compile the detailed sheets that go to an Examination Committee or whatever the body may be called. Since an external examiner has to be present at the meeting of the Examination Committee, a common scrutiny across all results follows automatically. Given then that there is one system within an institution for dealing with academic results, there is no problem of relating AP(E)L to the institution's quality assurance mechanisms. One size fits all.

In all this there is one important warning: portfolios. A portfolio is the standard way of compiling a set of learning claims. In some cases it is also a convenient way of supplying supporting evidence. But a portfolio is not the only way of supplying supporting evidence. There can be tests, examination papers to answer, interviews and so on. This battery of possible assessment instruments available relates to the warning concerning the size of a portfolio. Too often it can contain a mass of material which is descriptive rather than a tightly composed account of the learning which is being claimed, and all too often that is accompanied by a mass of evidence which at its kindest is not necessary to support the claim. This is because for quite understandable reasons individual applicants for credit for experiential learning both want and need to make the best possible showing. The solution to this potential problem is that in the interests of both student and academic there needs to be firm instruction and a clear set of rules as to the way portfolios are to be composed and submitted. That is in the interest of students so that they do not waste time and effort. It is vital for academic assessors because it keeps the tasks within reasonable boundaries. It avoids what some Americans refer to wryly as 'assessment by the wheelbarrow'. And from this the advantages of a central office are obvious. Along with all the other institutional rules and regulations for the assessment of prior experiential learning firm guidance needs to be given to the construction of portfolios.

Staff development is a natural corollary to these questions of academic organisation and procedures, assessment and quality assurance. At this stage the only thing to be said about it at present is that it is essential. Put differently, it is irresponsible for an institution to introduce AP(E)L unless it has made careful preparations. That means establishing suitable ways of familiarising those who are going to undertake the work both in theory and in practice with some of the more obvious implications. More than that though, it tends to lead to discussion of wider institutional matters than AP(E)L: admissions, grading, the curriculum, pedagogy, academic structures, all can come pouring out once AP(E)L is being done for real.

The most intractable aspect of AP(E)L is money. Who pays? Times have changed from the early days in the 1980s when the full range of AP(E)L services were made available without any thought of charging for them. In these 'price ticket on everything' days extending into the new century that cannot be. Broadly there are three possible and differing approaches to paying for the services on offer. For institutions with a credit accumulation system one solution is to include in the schedule of modules one which, whatever it is called – say Making Experience Count – is a credit-bearing course which enables people to reflect on their experience and produce learning claims with the requisite evidence all ready for assessment. Successful competition means that the individuals receive credit for completing the course, and in addition to whatever AP(E)L credit tutors have awarded. This way the course is included in the standard funding from the Higher Education Funding Council for England.

Institutions need have no hesitation in following this line. There is ample evidence to show that the intellectual demands on students who follow such a course are at least equivalent to those made on students following other courses. Were that not to be the case, it is unthinkable that the University of Nottingham would have introduced such a course to its regular programme.

Another approach is to unbundle the entire set of services into guidance, tutoring, assessment, and set a fee on each based on some calculation of the amount of an academic's time required to provide the service. In the unbundled approach there are examples of charges being levied for the amount of credit awarded either at so much a credit or rounded up into some stepped charge. That always seems a very dubious, even dangerous way of calculating fees and dues. It opens an institution to the charge of selling academic credit, unless the arrangements make it transparently clear that that is not the case.

A third way is to offer a Making Experience Count kind of course through adult education or whatever institutional agency copes with provision for the locality, and charge for it accordingly as for any other course on offer.

All that applies to regular enrolled students. Where an institution includes AP(E)L in its contracted services with an employer, its costs can be absorbed in an overall consultancy of service fee.

There is, however, another twist to the ways and means of paying for AP(E)L services. The most expensive item in the cost list is the academic tutor. Academics' time is expensive. AP(E)L can mop up inordinate amounts of time if it is allowed to do so. In the beginning that was precisely what happened and it created the impression that AP(E)L was too expensive to handle. But that is not necessarily so. The obvious way of limiting the amount of time academics spend on AP(E)L is to make sure that they handle academic matters and not administrative matters. This goes back to the advantages of a central unit. University administrative offices are quite capable of dealing with initial inquiries, first line guidance and advice about the suitability of AP(E)L for the inquirer and so on. Equipped with the information on a set of forms which inquirers are required to complete, administrators can also take things to a stage where a file can be sent to an academic so that at a glance it is obvious whether or not this particular candidate is ripe for AP(E)L. Thus cost savings are considerable.

These then are some of the issues and implications for institutions and their academics that have had to be faced when an AP(E)L scheme was introduced in institutions throughout the land at undergraduate and graduate level. In principle many of them, if not all, will crop up as institutions come to terms with some of the provisions for the Institute of Learning and Teaching. Coming to terms with AP(E)L can be a tedious business like any other academic innovation. But it can also be fun. Many a tutor has felt that AP(E)L has been a welcome stimulus, even a blood transfusion to academic life. And if it can be fun then almost inevitably students will learn more and learn it better.

5   Getting going

After the quiet, the activity. In the summer of 1999 after its official establishment that spring the ILT issued a series of documents which embodied the decisions taken by what had been the planning group but was now acting as a transitional board of the ILT. These documents laid out procedures for applying for the accreditation of an institutional programme, and of key importance for the theme of this story, a detailed set of the requirements to be met for experienced staff using what was called a fast track in line with one of the Booth group's recommendations. They amount to a set of ways and means of tackling the improvement of learning and teaching.

The ILT listed five routes to membership:

1 Institutional staff development programmes.
2 Institutional evaluation of portfolios.
3 Programmes validated by other approved agencies.
4 ILT evaluation of portfolios.
5 Initial entry route for experienced staff (available for two years).

The first route implies that an institution has submitted its programme for accreditation by the ILT and been successful. The second implies that the institution itself has been accredited by the ILT and so in a way acts as its agent for evaluating portfolios submitted for membership by its own staff. The third is essentially a way of incorporating within the ILT's activities the comparatively large number of institutions already operating the SEDA Teacher Accreditation Scheme. It also holds open the possibility for institutions which do not want to get involved directly with the ILT to make use of facilities present in other institutions. The fourth preserves the right of individuals to approach the ILT direct if for any reason they prefer to bypass their employing institution. And the fifth, of course, is the fast track recommended by the Booth Committee.

Towards institutional accreditation

From 2001 onwards the operational connection between AP(E)L and the ILT takes on an organised permanence in place of the temporary fast track arrangement. From then on academics and learning support staff will be able to seek membership by one of two routes, first mapped out by the Booth planning group. Either they can follow a programme devised and validated by their own university or college or a collaborating institution and accredited by the ILT or they can go down the AP(E)L route. In both cases evidence will be required of satisfactory achievement under the five headings of responsibility used through the negotiations which led to the establishment of the ILT in the first place:

1 Teaching and/or supporting learning in higher education.
2 Contribution to the design and planning of learning activities and/or programmes of study.
3 Provision of feedback and assessment of students' learning.
4 Contribution to the development of effective learning environments and student support systems.
5 Reflection on personal practice in teaching and learning and work to improve the teaching process.

And individuals can always apply directly to the ILT without making an application through their own institution.

Gone are the twenty-four items with their columns of detailed requirements. Gone too, for the present at any rate, is the Associate Membership.

The briefing from the ILT, Guidelines on Institutional Programme Accreditation, describes what it means by an accredited course. It includes taught elements and provides the knowledge and abilities which meet the requirements for the membership of the ILT as set out above. That amounts to Route 1. Route 2 as an accredited route or pathway is described as a set of activities which together accumulate evidence that the requirements for membership have been met. This route need not include taught courses but is expected to involve formal assessment of the evidence submitted against the ILT's requirements for membership. Route 2 is, as can be readily seen, is implying that AP(E)L is an accepted means of following that route.

The requirements of the course are set out quite expansively. Emphasis is put on 'disciplined and reflective approach(es) to the practice of teaching and the support of learning in higher education'. Applicants for membership are expected to show 'sufficient knowledge of generic pedagogical issues' to enable them to develop teaching and assessment strategies suitable for the students they teach. The ILT does not neglect formal disciplines. It says that: 'Programmes are expected to encourage the exploration of issues particular to differing disciplines.'

This does not mean, however, that the two routes are mutually exclusive. Route 2 can be taken down Route 1. It will be open to men and women with three years or more experience, either to produce evidence to show that the accredited programme has been completed satisfactorily without actually having followed it, or to produce evidence based on their experience which covers the five headings of responsibility on which the entire enterprise is based. AP(E)L again.

Indeed, the ILT knows full well that the diversity which exists among higher education institutions means that it is only common sense for universities and colleges to develop those approaches to the ILT requirements which are most appropriate to them, the academics and support staff who work within them, rather than trying to impose a template which applies to all. Provided that the five broad areas quoted above are met, all is well. And the ILT goes further in its wish to demonstrate that it means what it says about flexibility. Commenting on those five areas it says that it has no wish to constrain institutions from offering programmes with a distinctive focus such as 'learning technologies, student centred learning, workplace learning or action research'.

Again as evidence to prove what it means about flexibility, it accepts that existing well-established postgraduate courses may need no more than a brief documentary submission.

What it does insist on, and shows common sense speaking out in a civilised way, is that whether it is course or a pathway there needs to be an obvious coherence to the whole, that it has clear and achievable aims and objectives which are thoroughly understood by any staff who contribute to the programme. The central values listed already need to underpin the whole as they are implied broadly in the five areas of study. Clearly, no self-respecting tutor can fail to know the subject discipline backwards. The ILT 's purposes are highlighted when it says that tutors need to be able to use teaching methods which are appropriate both to the subject and the level at which it is being taught. It pushes pedagogical issues further by saying that its values include an understanding of students' learning styles, how to use learning technologies where they are appropriate, and an ability to monitor and evaluate their own teaching in the light of an understanding of the implications of quality assurance. The submission has to show that quality assurance is safeguarded through procedures which outline specific criteria and are subject to both internal and external moderation.

Formal accreditation procedure includes all the elements institutions have become well accustomed to, especially if they were previously associated with the Council for National Academic Awards (CNAA). Full documents have to be sent to the ILT for preliminary consideration dealing with the programme outline itself, the staffing and resources available. Queries, if any, are then dealt with. An institutional visit follows by a duly appointed panel of ILT accreditors. Their report goes to the Accrediting Committee of the ILT having been commented on by the institution applying for accreditation. There a decision is taken as to whether to award accreditation or not and sent to the head of the institution and the course team. The claim is that the entire procedure takes up to four months.

It is worth lingering a little to list the requirements of SEDA for its Teacher Accreditation Scheme which was established long before there was any mention of an Institute of Learning and Teaching. Its pamphlet on *The Accreditation of Teachers in Higher Education* lists seven professional values:

- understanding how students learn;
- recognising individuals' differences in learning;
- concern for students' development;
- commitment to scholarship;
- collaborative working/ability to work in a team;
- practising equal opportunities;
- continuing reflection on professional practice.

It requires an accredited teacher to show how these principles and values underpin day-to-day work. They are more or less the same as those for the ILT. When it comes to outcomes there is about the same overlap between what the ILT calls its six items of core knowledge and what SEDA calls its eight outcomes. The ILT lists:

1 The subject material that they will be teaching.
2 Appropriate methods for teaching and learning in the subject area and at the level of the academic programme.

3 Models of how students learn, both generically and in their subject.
4 The use of learning technologies appropriate to the context in which they teach.
5 Methods for monitoring and evaluating their own teaching.
6 The implications of quality assurance for practice.

SEDA lists:

1 Design a teaching programme from a course outline, document or syllabus.
2 Use a wide variety and appropriate range of teaching and learning methods effectively and efficiently to work with large groups, small groups and one-to-one.
3 Provide support to students on academic and pastoral matters.
4 Use a wide range of assessment techniques to assess student work and to enable students to monitor their own progress.
5 Use a range of self, peer and student monitoring and evaluation techniques.
6 Perform effectively the teaching support and academic administrative tasks involved in the teaching in the department of the institution.
7 Develop personal and professional coping strategies within the constraints and opportunities of the institutional setting.
8 Reflect on personal and professional practice and development, assess their future development needs, and make a plan for their continuing professional development.

Of course there are differing emphases to be found in the two systems. But the broad brush agreement over the essential knowledge requirements and the professional value criteria make is easy to understand why the ILT gives automatic accreditation to approved SEDA schemes. Similarly, the procedure is broadly the same for approving a SEDA scheme as for accreditation by the ILT. So it is no surprise that institutions with existing SEDA approved schemes are in no hurry to seek accreditation directly from the ILT, although most of them will have to do so by 2002 since that is when the retrospective approval runs out for SEDA programmes which were a going concern before the advent of the ILT. Some such institutions are revising their SEDA schemes for a renewed approval rather than go direct to the ILT. And some universities without a formal staff development programme are preferring to go down the SEDA route rather than approach the ILT at this time.

It is important to put in context the overlap between the ILT and SEDA. In June 2000 SEDA had a publicly available list which showed that it had recognised forty-seven programmes in the UK under its Teacher Accreditation Scheme, with a further seven programmes recognised overseas and ten programmes recognised through its Associate Teacher Scheme. At that date the ILT showed on its Website that it had given retrospective approval to forty-one of those programmes to run through until 2002 when re-accreditation would be required. The missing six are those that had not at that date sought retrospective approval but may well do so in the future.

A closer look at those respective lists set out in Table 5.1 below reveals some interesting sidelights on the overall issue of staff development in higher education to which the Dearing proposal for an ILT offered a substantial boost. For convenience the older universities have been grouped as Pre-1992 whether they are ancient, former municipal, former CAT or Robbins. The former polytechnics are grouped as Post-1992. The colleges are variously University College or Colleges of Higher Education, and the specialist colleges referred to are the London College of Fashion, the British School of Osteopathy, the Central School of Speech and Drama.

Far from it being the case then that the older universities were lagging behind in staff development, it emerges that half as many of the pre-1992 universities as the post-1992 universities had sought SEDA approval. And when those figures are carried through to the ILT approval column it shows that all eleven of them were anxious to make their number with the ILT, whereas six of the post-1992 universities had not made their move for retrospective approval.

Those numbers conceal the many individual academics who have been accredited through following successfully a SEDA approved programme. There were 1,763 in all of which 1,444 are in British institutions and 369 are for members of overseas institutions. How those numbers are distributed between the categories of institutions listed

Table 5.1 Approved colleges and universities

SEDA approvals	ILT retrospective approvals	
Pre-1992 Universities	11	11
Post-1992 Universities	28	22
Colleges of HE	5	6
Specialist Colleges	3	2
Totals	47	41

above cannot be told, but whichever way they are regarded it all
amounts to an impressive record of continuing professional development which was a fully operational voluntary scheme.

The number and institutional coverage of those figures indicate a
substantial state of readiness on the part of many universities and
colleges to align themselves with the overall purposes of the ILT.
Looked at in a different way, however, the story is not quite so
encouraging. This relates to AP(E)L which is bound to feature in
accredited submissions in the future. A different way of considering
the preparedness of institutions for the ILT is to ask how many of
those featuring in Table 5.1 are ready and able to develop procedures
for AP(E)L. There can be no absolutely reliable answers to that
question. The nearest approach to it is to read off those numbers
against some from the Mapping Exercise referred to before. Of the
eleven pre-1992 universities seven claimed in their return to the Trust
that they had AP(E)L policies either at departmental or institutional
level. Fourteen of the twenty-two post-1992 universities also made
that claim. So did two of the Colleges of HE. In the context of some
130 higher education institutions on the Higher Education Funding
Council's list that leaves quite a distance to go before it can be said
that the geographical spread of AP(E)L facility is adequate.

One curious remark in the ILT briefing paper on accreditation is this:
'Accredited courses may lead to an award offered by the institution but
courses which are not award bearing may also be accredited provided
they meet the accreditation criteria.' This is stating the obvious. It is no
business of the ILT to do more than point to the obvious possibility of
an overlap between courses submitted to it for accreditation and their
suitability or otherwise for inclusion in an institution's scheme of postgraduate awards. It does however draw attention to one result of the
ILT's arrival. It is back to the carrot and stick balance. Any institution
has to answer as best it can the question: 'Why should academics in this
institution bother with the ILT?'

It can try to answer that in several ways. It can make it a requirement
that newly appointed staff undertake the institution's arrangements for
seeking membership of the ILT, whether that be through an accredited
programme, through the institution's evaluation of portfolios or
through some collaboration with another institution. It can make
membership a requirement for completing a probationary period. It
can assume that the fast track will have soaked up most of the experienced staff in mid career. But as a long-term settled requirement it needs
something more substantial to satisfy itself that it is making appropriate
provision.

One way to do that is to link an accredited ILT programme, whether Route 1 or Route 2, or a combination of the two, with a postgraduate scheme leading to a Master's degree. It enables the institution to offer its academics a postgraduate award which they understand full well, which has elements which happen to meet the membership requirements of the ILT. It can assign a credit value at M level to the ILT programme whatever it is. The ILT gains too because sailing under the academic flag of a university or college endows its award with an authority which it cannot have as a standalone qualification. All that is a matter for institutional decision.

As for individual academics, as the word got around their institutions about the ILT and what was in store, some of those who were reasonably experienced with a few years of higher education teaching behind them began to tot up the score for themselves. If the 'norm' came to mean anything then to have an ILT membership on a CV could do no harm and might possibly become a telling issue. It could even become an issue within their own institution. So although it could hardly be said that there was great enthusiasm among established academic staff at the prospect of seeking membership of the ILT for many at worst there was a resigned acceptance and at best some professional sense of welcoming proper recognition of their work. Of course there was certainly some strong individual resistance to what could be interpreted as an impertinent motion of no confidence by interfering busybodies. But even the most cynical had to recognise that, like it or not, the ILT existed and had to be taken into account.

These then were the circumstances under which institutions took decision as to whether to submit direct to the ILT programmes for accreditation, whether to continue to use an existing SEDA programme which had been developed and carried current accreditation, or whether just to wait and see.

6   Some flavours of institutional accredited courses

All institutional decisions are bound to be influenced by their history, their academic standing, their sense of purpose, the relationship existing between research and teaching as they perceive it and indeed all that goes up to make the culture which gives any institution its distinctiveness. Like everything else then submissions for ILT accreditation will reflect those institutional characteristics. Inevitably, necessarily and properly, institutions take different approaches to meeting the requirements for an accredited ILT course leading to membership, or for a programme leading to a SEDA Certificate of Accreditation for Teachers in Higher Education which currently carries eligibility for ILT membership with it. What is clear is that gone are the days when a brief syllabus outline sufficed. Booklets and handbooks are the rule with comprehensive information about organisational issues, the course tutors involved and how to contact them, tutorial and guidance arrangements, course management and a detailed timetable of meetings all in addition to a full exposition of the course components, their learning intentions and the assessment procedures associated with them. Many then add clear instructions as to how to present the necessary evidence. And some are sweetly inviting: 'We are sure that you will benefit from participating in all of the sessions time-tabled for the first year.' It is a bit like a promise of tea or something stronger if the carefully considered directions as how to get there are followed. In themselves though these documents and handbooks serve as splendid examples of how to set about designing and implementing a course in ways calculated to reassure likely participants and encourage them to stay the course. Anyone who can do that needs no prompting about how to serve students.

However, there are several important differences in emphasis between some of those programmes. Those that are planned as development programmes for new and novice teachers who may or may not find the course is a required component of a probationary year, tend to be characterised by formal learning and teaching practices more didactic than others with detailed hand holding about every aspect of the course. That is not true of all courses for beginning teachers. Right from the beginning explicitly some seek to promote a critical self-analysis of the candidate's day-to-day work as a self-assessment habit, relying on systematic reflection of their experience. Those that have a catch-all intention, suitable for both novices and their more experienced colleagues, tend to have a deliberate balance between the instructional and the reflective. Some offer two different courses, one for novices and one for the experienced. Some are linked to a modular Master's degree. There are book lists, glossaries and handbooks representing a very large investment of tutorial time and reprographic resources. Some use the first person throughout, addressing potential participants directly. And some handbooks are complete with timetables and dates laying out the full sequence of requirements.

There are different requirements laid on participants for submission and completion. Some treat the programme like a regular course and so everything to do with assessment comes at its end. Others have three or four submission dates during the academic year. Others again take the work in progress as both formative and summative assessment. As implied above some programmes are linked through a credit accumulation scheme to a Master's degree, and within that the speed of completion depends on the number of modules that an individual academic can fit into the plethora of other academic tasks now to be met. This is applying to academic staff the 'student paced' approach to learning programmes.

The use of language varies too. In some information packs for potential participants the language is quite formal, whereas in others the use of the first person goes the full distance in creating a friendly supportive context for the programme. Glossaries are included in some Users Handbooks and all have book lists running from a few for essential reading through to comprehensive lists which would not disgrace a library.

What is absolutely clear is that institutions have invested very large resources in this form of staff development. Quite apart from the staffing of the courses and all the administration, record keeping, assessment and committee work which inevitably is involved with any academic programme these days, an incalculable number of hours and days have gone into the design and creation of the handbooks which are part and parcel of every course. This is even more notable where a handbook includes a whole range of blank forms for participants to complete so that they act as an unofficial and undeclared set of do's and don'ts for the entire enterprise.

As its name implies, as the Staff and Educational Development Association (SEDA) promoted and supported by staff developers in their institutions, some programmes tend to put greater emphasis on the classroom competence of teachers in higher education than on the subject expertise in the content of what is taught. Notwithstanding this some SEDA courses lay heavy and deliberate emphasis on the teaching of different subjects, rooting everything else in them as a matter of professional principle.

Something of this variety which exists already can be deduced from the titles of the programmes which the ILT has approved retrospectively. There are Postgraduate Certificates in Teaching and Learning; Postgraduate Professional Certificate in Learning and Teaching; Postgraduate Certificate in Teaching in Higher Education; Postgraduate Certificate in Academic Practice; Postgraduate Certificate in Education and Professional Development; Postgraduate Certificate in Further and Higher Education Programme for Staff with Teaching Responsibility; Postgraduate Certificate in Educational Development; Staff Development Programme Accreditation of Teachers in Higher Education; Advanced Diploma in Professional Development – teaching and learning in HE; Postgraduate Certificate in Academic Practice; Certificate in Teaching in HE; Teaching and Learning Programme; University's Accreditation scheme; Teacher Accreditation Course.

What cannot be known at this stage is how institutions and the ILT will view programmes when the fast track arrangements for experienced academics runs out in 2001. A good deal then will depend on the Continuing Professional Development programmes which individuals follow to remain in good standing with the ILT itself. Perhaps more significantly once the fast track has run its course and brought into membership relatively large numbers of experienced academics, time will tell what use then will be made of AP(E)L. No doubt some institutions will take seriously the Dearing notion of the 'norm' – all HE teachers to have gone through an accredited programme – so that the AP(E)L provision will need to be available for academic and support staff who are appointed from a different institution or enter higher education teaching from a profession or business or industry bringing with them substantial experience which could well yield knowledge and skill which fitted some parts of the ILT programme.

Others no doubt will take the Dearing 'norm' as a piece of pious, unrealisable and unnecessary rhetoric and rest content with using ILT membership as an element in the probationary period.

What cannot be said and would be a travesty of the truth to assert is that there is a neat division between the younger universities who are eager beavers for this form of staff development and older universities who treat the whole thing as a bore and chore to be dealt with as expeditiously as possible to conform with current requirements. The figures in the SEDA and ILT lists on page 62 are more than numbers. They represent a commitment of all the institutions cited there which runs way beyond paper conformity.

But as the range of titles just quoted shows, there is a substantial variety in the programmes already approved to support the ILT's claim that it cares more for diversity than conformity.

For example, within the outline format of the five ILT requirements, one institution chose to organise its submission for accreditation in three sections for what it called its Postgraduate Certificate in Learning and Teaching in Higher Education. The first was the Practice of Teaching in HE. The second was IT and Resource-Based Learning, and the third was Contextual Issues on HE. The pages in the course handbook for each has sections on aims, learning objectives, syllabus outline, strategies for learning and teaching and scheduled activities, assessment, and an indicative reading list. Reading those courses off against the fivefold requirements of the ILT, it is easy to see that the flexibility the ILT proclaims is there for the taking. In that case the flexibility in design is mirrored by flexibility in provision. Note the discrete introduction of AP(E)L. 'You may . . . wish to explore the possibility of getting some credit for learning you have done previously, and if you have not already done so please contact the course coordinator as soon as possible. 'This is AP(E)L by another name. But it is extremely interesting and a deft way of introducing the topic. Right from the beginning of the 1980s the words, 'the assessment of prior and experiential learning' lie awkwardly on the tongue and uneasily in the head. Here a sensible way of getting round that problem is used to indicate to tutors that there are other ways of meeting requirements than attending a course and sitting in a classroom. Jargon is eschewed. Nowhere in the documents does the label AP(E)L appear. Despite the fact this institution makes substantial use of AP(E)L for its students.

The developmental flavour of this ILT accredited programme comes over strongly. In the introduction this appears: 'We have built into the course opportunities for you to put into practice what you are learning and to develop learning plans according to subject specific needs.' Later there is a page headed 'Identifying Personal Teaching Development Needs'. This is couched in an easy conversational style as befits the purpose of the section which may be unfamiliar to many; to invite reflection on present strengths and weaknesses at the beginning of the course as the reference point for further reflection on performance later on. There is another section headed 'Teaching Observation Reports: Notes for Guidance'. Observation of a teacher is part of the course. The ten items running from 'Preparation' through 'Suitability of material' to 'Other Comments' gives applicants a strong steer as to what is required of them and presumably offers assessors a common framework for assessment, just as there are pages of advice as to how to organise the 'Assignment Presentation and the criteria which will be used for its assessment'.

The subtitle to the course is 'Part of an accredited Continuing Professional Development framework leading to an MA award for teachers in Higher Education.' Twenty credits are awarded for the first of the three courses with ten credits each for the other two, making forty credits in all towards the necessary total of eighty. As with many postgraduate programmes it is organised on a credit accumulation system so that a tutor can spread the numbers of units taken over longer than two semesters, according to the day-to-day workload.

This is a friendly document, unthreatening, designed no doubt to allay the fears of sceptics. More importantly, it manages throughout to convey the intention of supporting tutors' professional development through their own self-assessment while in no way providing heavy handed *ex cathedra* scrutiny.

A different way of approaching the staff development programme for beginning teachers is to divide the curriculum into six sections designed to meet the ILT requirements overall.

1 Understanding Higher Education.
2 Teaching for Learning in Higher Education.
3 Academic Support for Students.
4 Assessment in Higher Education.
5 Curriculum Design, Development, Evaluation and Quality Assurance.
6 Educational Resources and Technology; theory and practice.

Each is treated as a discrete course deliberately so, calculated to be helpful for beginning teachers, given all the other preoccupations they have. Interestingly, while this programme is available to experienced academic staff, the rubric says that it is anticipated that experienced colleagues will prefer to apply direct to the ILT for membership. But whoever takes this Postgraduate Certificate in Learning and Teaching (Higher Education) as it is called, can score 60 academic credit points at Master's level.

The course details also emphasise that each participant will have mentoring support from a colleague in their own department or discipline. Further, those mentors will receive training and the mentoring will form an official part of their teaching load. During an academic year each mentor gets an allowance of 13 hours for each mentee. It is comparatively rare to find commitments like that set out so firmly in the details which are circulated to academic and support staff. It sends a clear message about the institution commitment to staff development.

A SEDA approved course in a different institution calls its programme a Postgraduate Certificate/Diploma in Higher Education. It is organised on a credit accumulation system where 35 credits are required for a Certificate and 70 for a Diploma. There are three core modules, all three of which are required to be taken by newly appointed staff and the second and third for experienced academics. They are The Effective Practitioner; The Reflective Practitioner; and Professional Practice. The rest of the programme is made up of modules selected from a further eight: Application of Learning Theory; Assessment of Learning; Curriculum Design and Quality Management; Computer-Based Learning Resources; Interpersonal Skills; the New Academic; Project (for Diploma only); and Research Methods – this must be taken by candidates taking the project module.

The Participant's Handbook asserts that 'SEDA Principles, Values and Objectives form a sympathetic interface with the aims of the course'. This is obvious from the Aims section in the Handbook.

- To provide an understanding of how students learn, the impact of their individual differences, means to assist the development of their responsibility for their own learning and professional competence and the realisation of equal opportunities.
- To enhance the skills as curriculum designers, teachers, guides to learning and assessors, in the context of translating an understanding of educational theories into relevant higher education experience.
- To establish the value and methods on continued reflection on professional practice, including a commitment to team working, scholarship, searching for continuous improvement in teaching and sharing good practice.
- To encourage the attainment of individual accreditation by SEDA.

The Handbook goes to some lengths to explain the possibilities for obtaining credit either for prior or experiential learning or both; how to set about it; how to get professional help in organising evidence derived either from study (prior) or from experience; how to make a claim and how that claim is assessed. All that occurs within the institution's regulations and standard assessment and quality assurance systems. They stipulate that the maximum amount of credit for prior and experiential learning is 20 for the Certificate and 35 for the Diploma, being 50% in either case.

Every module is described in terms of its aims, learning outcomes, content, the teaching and learning methods to be used, how the assessment is conducted, examples of how to organise the elements of a portfolio and an indicative reading list. The Participant's Handbook stands as a first-rate learner's guide. Further, in making explicit the possibilities available for gaining credit on the basis of experiential learning it is deliberately broadening the potential base for its internal recruitment.

The A4 sized pamphlet with six folded pages is attached to the Handbook of Guidance for the SEDA/ILT programme offered in one of the top research universities in the country. There are five components to this programme:

1 A series of workshops provided by the staff of the training unit.
2 A teaching portfolio developed by the individual.
3 Mentoring support provided by the department.
4 Monitoring and review carried out by the department.
5 Assessment by the portfolio assessment panel.

As if to indicate the status of this programme, the first pages in the Handbook give the composition of the assessment panel, including the external examiner and a list of some nineteen senior academics who form the programme's Steering Committee, both being chaired by the same Pro Vice Chancellor.

The pamphlet outlines the four elements to assessment:

1 Self-assessment in the form of reflection on work and a plan of continuing professional development activities.
2 Peer assessment of the process of mapping the portfolio evidence on the SEDA objectives and values.
3 Regular Head of Department monitoring and review.
4 Assessment of the portfolio by a panel of senior colleagues.

The second of these four elements is covered on a full page in tabular form for each of the eight objectives listed as requirements for a SEDA approved programme. Each has three columns:

• Tasks and responsibilities relevant to SEDA objectives.
• Appropriate portfolio evidence.
• Reflection relevant to SEDA values.

For instance, the first entry on the page for Objective 1 – Design a teaching programme or scheme of work from a course outline, document or syllabus. Under tasks and responsibilities relevant to SEDA objectives, this appears:

> Specify the rationale and intended learning outcomes for a particular course or course component.

Under appropriate portfolio evidence, the table says:

> A short statement on the rationale on the chosen course.

Under reflection relevant to SEDA values, this is the entry:

> In reflecting on your evidence you should be able to demonstrate a professional level of critical appraisal.

In this way the Handbook works through each objective so that participants have in effect an *aide mèmoire* for the entire course. This is supported by a number of blank forms for completion, covering each of the objectives so that candidates can be in no doubt what it being asked of them.

This is a model of clarity and there are two outstanding and somewhat unusual features within it. The first is that the programme is taken at a relatively slow pace compared with many others. For new lecturers 'the scheme is intended to run concurrently with a three-year probationary period' but if an individual has a limited range of teaching responsibilities at the beginning of the probationary period it may make sense to delay enrolment. Established staff then may either follow the three-year sequence or base their submission on a combination of material drawn from the previous three years and concurrent experience.

The other unusual feature to this programme appears in the first element of assessment quoted above: '. . . and a plan of continuing professional development activities.'

For probationary novices to have such a requirement laid upon them, to think ahead to their future needs and reflect on them as part of their self-assessment right at the beginning of their experience as teachers in higher education, is not only demanding for them as individuals: it also shows that the culture of the institution encourages that kind of imaginative professionalism.

This contrasts sharply with the culture of another distinguished research university. There the Staff Development Officer would be laughed out of court at any attempt to introduce a formal programme. Conversations with individuals about problems create some kind of network of academics who are interested in teaching, learning and curricula issues, and that is as far as internal provision goes for professional development. Dearing's 'norm' is unlikely to become the order of the day there.

Another SEDA approved programme takes a different approach to meet the requirements. It is called a Postgraduate Certificate in Learning and Teaching in Higher Education. It is mandatory for newly appointed academic staff to undertake the course and open to others.

The stated aims of this programme are:

- To equip you with the basic pedagogical tools essential to support active learning and to create an effective learning environment.
- To introduce theories of learning, teaching and assessment and encourage their appropriate application in teaching practice through a deep understanding and critical evaluation.
- To provide a programme which develops in you the habits of a reflective professional practitioner.
- To enable you to achieve the standard of professional practice required for national accreditation as a teacher in higher education.

This section of the Participant's Handbook is headed Course Aims and Learning Outcomes. However, instead of digging into the jargon of Learning Outcomes this is what follows that statement of aims:

On successful completion of the Postgraduate Certificate in Learning and Teaching in Higher Education you will be able to:

Provide a portfolio of evidence of practice and critical reflection which meets the criteria for teacher accreditation in higher education.
Learn from observation of others and feedback on observation of your own practice by peers, mentors and tutors.
Describe how theories of learning and teaching relate to your own professional judgements and practice.
Design, deliver and evaluate a teaching programme in a way which reflects SEDA values and principles (they are listed later in the Handbook).
Appropriately assess students' work in line with University regulations and in a way which reflects SEDA values and principles.
Understand the current context of teaching in higher education and be familiar with basic C and IT for use in learning and teaching in higher education.

This gear shift down to earthy language about what the course will enable newly appointed staff to do, is a refreshing way to set about engaging them from the beginning when they have many other things to think about. And to underline the intentions informing the course, in the Welcome section great emphasis is put on the development of reflective practitioners as a trailer for the prominence given to just that in both aims and outcomes. And that reflection is put in context right away:

The course is open to participants from different subject disciplines who will bring with them a variety of backgrounds and a broad range of professional practice and teaching traditions. The course both acknowledges and makes use of this diversity to enrich the discussions on models of effective learning, teaching and assessment.

Through using the first person in addressing participants either actual or potential the tone of the programme is established as essentially supportive. This is emphasised through the explanations given of what the experience of following the course will actually be.

The programme is made up of four modules: Introduction to Learning and Teaching in HE; development as a reflective practitioner; assessment in HE; and approaches to learning and teaching in HE. Each is conducted through a mixture of workshops either all day or half day, mentoring, teaching observation work-based learning and independent study.

It is the first of three courses organised on a credit accumulation basis where the second course leads to a Postgraduate Diploma and the third culminates in a Master's degree. So progression is built in. It is the first which results in SEDA teacher accreditation and with it eligibility for ILT membership. The Postgraduate Certificate attracts 48 credits, the Diploma 96 credits and the Master's degree gains 96 credits, making a total of 180 for the threefold programme.

Earlier in the Handbook there is a section on Learning and Teaching Methods. The Kolb learning cycle is the basis of the entire operation. Work-based learning 'involves you in building a portfolio of evidence of developing professional practice as a teacher in HE'. Action Learning then appears as the main engine of learning. 'You will be assigned a learning set which will support your work on the programme and members of your set will act as peer assessors for your portfolio.' Ten lines then describe what action learning actually is, and in different language it is essentially an account of the assessment of experiential learning with a very important caveat: 'The set is less concerned with personal development and discovery than with learning and action. Put simply, it is about solving problems and getting things done.'

This is followed by a paragraph on independent study, with the responsibility for its effectiveness put firmly on the participant. 'This programme relies heavily on your resourcefulness as an independent learner.' And despite the resources made available through the regular conduct of the course: 'However, you will need to access additional resources to support your own independent learning. Moreover it is this independent learning which develops your understanding of learning and teaching needs for underpinning with scholarship.' The roles of mentors and course tutors are laid out as if for the purposes of peer observation.

Participants are then treated to detailed accounts of the methods of assessment for all four modules where a portfolio has to be compiled containing the various items listed. For example, for the Assessment in Higher Education module the portfolio entries need to include:

- examples of your approach to formative and summative assessment – two of each;
- a critical analysis of your current assessment practice in relation to learning theory;
- examples of existing or planned innovation in your assessment strategy including an educational rationale for these;
- reflections on what student assessment results tell you about the effectiveness of your teaching.

The first aim listed for this programme begins 'to equip you with the basic pedagogical tools essential . . .' By the end of the programme it is not easy to see what tools have been omitted. This example brings out more clearly than some the developmental aspect of CPD. It does so because while there is a hierarchy of conceptual progression running through the four modules, the responsibility for reflection and independent study rests firmly on the academics following the course. The implicit message is 'do unto students as is done to you'.

Another university describes its Advanced Certificate in Higher Education Practice as 'a discussion-based enquiry-led introduction to educational issues for those engaged in academic work'. The course aim is set out thus:

> The course aims to develop participants' effectiveness as academics working in higher education. This includes extending their skills, knowledge and imagination as teachers, course planners, advisors and supervisors, research colleagues and administrators. The course aim is to help each participant develop the quality of their professional practice through a process of enquiry and to provide opportunities to discuss issues across disciplines and professions as part of a collegial group.
>
> The course carries with it 30 M level credits. In addition to the 60 hours contact time the expectation is that as much time will be spent on action orientated research in the workplace. This will include carrying out observational tasks and making regular contributions to email discussions.

That has a very different flavour to it compared with the others noted already. However, its explicit concentration on aspects of individual professional development, as in 'developing the imagination' is accompanied by firm institutional requirements. New academic staff on probation are required to attend the course. Successful completion of the course will be taken into consideration at the end of the three-year probation period. However, it is interesting to note that 'the School will remain responsible for the recommendation to the Promotions Committee as regards research performance, administrative capability and competence to teach the discipline'. The timed sessions run over eight months beginning in September and including two weekend residential meetings. But the course itself comprises an intensive beginning covering a general introduction, teaching learning in higher education, assessment issues, teaching and research and administration; the nature of work in the contemporary university summed up by a presentation by the class. Curriculum and course design; the creation and management of learning follows at the first residential meeting. The second residential is devoted to the development of a portfolio, issues in supervision and research management. Completed portfolios have to be submitted by the end of August.

The course details list for the possible content on a portfolio: a video of a class plus analytical account; a critical account of an example of change of management; a teaching log; a referred journal article, a study focused on a teaching and learning problem in a particular subject area. It is no surprise then to find that tucked away in the text, AP(E)L features: 'In certain circumstances it will be appropriate to take account of a participant's prior experience and the Institution is currently considering Accreditation of Prior Experiential Learning (AP(E)L) procedures.'

This is consistent with the course's methodology.

> The course will be practice based . . . Course members will identify issues and concerns in their own practice and test the solutions they devise for resolving them. This will involve gathering and analysing evidence about their practices from the point of view of their students, their peers and themselves, negotiating problem-solutions with these parties and evaluating their effectiveness. Additionally High Tec is an integral part of the provision. Use of email listserv is central to the work of the course; for routine administrative issues and for sharing of observations, reports and the discussion of ideas.

This last requirement for participants to use email as part of the day-to-day operation of the course is another distinctive feature. It looks like a high tec version of the old adage – there is more than one way of killing a cat. Instead of providing a specific course for the development of high tec skills, the requirement to use them in order to follow the programme gets to the same destination without saying so. In itself that is a valuable lesson in staff development for anyone who cares to think about it.

Another version of a staff development programme leading to membership of the ILT is called Postgraduate Certificate in Learning and Teaching in Higher Education. It is organised in two parts, each part taking a year and each carrying 30 credits towards a Master's degree. If the workload of an individual makes it possible to complete the two parts in one year, the regulations permit that. That is the AP(E)L by another name. The course requirements are laid out under three headings: performance outcomes; knowledge outcomes; and professional values. Each of the first two are set out in tabular form divided into Part One and Part Two so that the requirements for Part Two can be seen as a progression from Part One. As to be expected, broadly all coincide with the fivefold pattern suggested by the Booth group and then adopted by the ILT. The professional values apply to Parts One and Two and show some difference of emphasis from some of the other examples. This section reads:

> For both Parts One and Two of the course you need to show how your professional practice is underpinned by your commitment to certain professional values namely:
> scholarship in teaching
> collegiality
> ensuring equality of educational opportunity.
> Continued reflection and consequent improvements in practice and respect for individual learners and for their development.

Equipped with all that information an intending applicant can decide whether it is the two-year or one-year programme which is most suitable. Not that that decision is the applicant's alone. Each student is assigned a tutor and a mentor. Right at the beginning of the course the student is required to write a Personal Position Statement. This is a kind of personal internal audit of what has been learned so far to match the course requirements, and then of what needs to be done to fill the gap of those items which have not been learned already; and very interestingly 'the possibilities, opportunities and limitations of your role in relation to the course'. That is followed by the composition of a Learning Agreement with the help of both tutor and mentor which outlines the learning intentions designed to meet the requirements of the course and how they are to be met over its duration. There is a third stage to this early planning. The Learning Agreement goes to the Course Committee for scrutiny and approval.

It is obvious that the role of the tutor and mentor is critical to this mental stock taking and mapping out future activities. So, as well as there being a Student Handbook there are separate guides to Producing a Position Statement, Producing a Learning Agreement, The Mentoring Relationship, and last Producing a Teaching Portfolio. This last is 'not only a product with contents, it entails processes of planning, preparing and evaluating your teaching . . . is to demonstrate your competence in teaching and we assess and accredit that competence'. And in quite explicit and fulsome style all that is unpacked so that no applicant let alone those on the course can be under any illusions of what is being expected of them. To what is perhaps in a more extended way than some of the other examples, this collection of documents and guidelines stands as an admirable version of what the academics on the course ought to go away from and do likewise for their own students.

Another institution takes a pincer grip on its programme. It is offered as a one-year commitment, and satisfactory completion is a requirement for all academic staff with less than five years' teaching experience in higher education. The blurb says that more experienced staff may find it 'a valuable and learning experience'. That institutional requirement is matched by another. The carrot follows the stick. Where attendance is obligatory, the home department is compensated financially. It is credited with 90 hours over the academic year at part-time lecturing rates on the assumption that the participant's teaching role will be reduced accordingly. For the individual the course carries with it within a credit accumulation scheme, 15 credits at level 3 and 30 credits at M level.

As a SEDA accredited course all its requirements are met and therefore for those of the ILT. But the language of the course aims and their description has a different emphasis from many. The course aims are listed as:

- to widen your repertoire and competence of teaching and assessment methods to support you in any teaching problems you face;
- to increase your understanding of teaching and learning processes so that you can make appropriate and informed decisions about course design and choice of teaching, learning and assessment methods;
- to foster the habit of reflective teaching and of professionalism in evaluating and improving teaching;
- to foster the development of a scholarly and research-based approach to teaching and learning in higher education;
- to help you become a more skilled and scholarly teacher in higher education.

Given the institution's pincer grip on the course the use of the first person to create a direct connection with participants establishes right from the beginning that the underlying purpose of the programme is to be personally supportive and encourage a developmental view of the academic tasks they are undertaking.

Kolb's Experiential Learning Cycle is set out in the section of course philosophy and rationale to underline some of the implications of those course aims.

A programme of workshops lays the ground for the entire enterprise but beyond that how the aims and objectives are met is up to the individual working with a tutor on a Learning Contract which is negotiated between them. In this particular programme emphasis is put on those negotiations being about whatever may be the most appropriate way of tackling the work in the light of the interests of the department of the participant and the disciplinary context for the teaching. Thus there is a greater prominence given explicitly to the learning and teaching in different subject disciplines than in many programmes.

Participants are required to write profiles of themselves and their work as 'a record of your ability/knowledge in specified areas at particular points in time. It represents how you view yourself in relation to a set of learning outcomes and enables you to see readily which areas you need to work on or develop'. The profiles go into a portfolio which form part of the assessment procedure. Self-assessment and peer learning features. At the final assessment as well as the portfolio there are taken into account three teaching observations conducted during the year, two of which are conducted by tutors and the third by a fellow course member, the two profiles, demonstration of the successful completion of agreed outcomes and what is called an Accreditation Interview. This last is essentially a two-way conversation, something like an appraisal. The applicant has the opportunity of presenting to the tutor supplementary evidence to expand the account give in the portfolio, and as a course completion occasion has the opportunity of reflecting on the experience of the course and 'celebrate your achievements'. The first person again.

This is all expanded in an extensive document which goes through every stage of the course as it develops and acts as a comprehensive guide to what an applicant is undertaking. It is CPD in its own right with plenty of inducements for taking it further as in the last aim already quoted: 'to help you become a more skilled and scholarly teacher of your discipline'.

The Participant's Handbook from another programme, the Advanced Diploma in Professional Development, begins with a section Who is it for? and explains that it is 'designed for newly appointed teachers and related staff with less than two years teaching experience in higher education'. And to be eligible an applicant needs to be either a full-time staff member of the university, or a part-timer with at least 6 hours teaching each week and in both cases holding 'a degree or equivalent professional qualification which recognises your subject expertise'.

The section on Course Philosophy and rationale indicates the programme is to:

> support teachers in a changing higher education environment and acts as a forum for debate on teaching and learning matters. It provides opportunities for a creative exchange of education ideas across faculties and between new teachers and more experienced colleagues.

It goes on:

> The theory of active or experiential learning seeks to encourage you to take responsibility for your own learning. The programme delivery has an emphasis on workshops and group learning by self-directed learning.

As a SEDA accredited course it covers all the expected course aims and is committed to SEDA's core values. It take two semesters to complete, requiring 360 hours of notional learning composed of 86 hours for developmental workshops and learning set meetings, 257 hours for practice work-based learning and private study, 8 hours for individual consultations with programme tutors and 9 hours for teaching observations.

Methodological explanations follow: workshops – 'a generic term for a range of learning activities' – action learning sets 'during an action set meeting each member is allocated time to present a problem' and other set members act as critics or enablers to help find a solution. Guidelines are given for managing a learning set, the role of the mentor as a device for keeping tuned to the needs of individual disciplines, how best to use action research for the development of teaching practice, observation of teaching, creating a learning log, and learning agreements. This last plays a key role in the programme since participants are required to complete a negotiated learning agreement for each of the eight objectives of the course, which reflect the SEDA requirements. Assessment is on a pass/fail basis. A portfolio is required to demonstrate evidence of having met the objectives set out in the learning agreements in two ways: reflection on the way in which the programme values relate to each of the learning outcomes undertaken; and samples of how the work was done and what it produced.

As a commentary to steer participants in the direction they are required to go, the rubric then says that the portfolio should aim to produce two categories of evidence:

> provide evidence for a systematic appraisal of your teaching competence, record your development through reflection and the evaluation of practice; demonstrate that you have achieved the programme's learning objectives.

At the back of the pack there is a collection of blank forms which participants have to complete as part of their work. It is not easy to see how this programme could be more supportive and helpful in enabling academic staff from all disciplines to acquire this diploma.

As another programme shows, by going modular instead of linear an institution can take full account of the varying workloads and domestic circumstances of some of its academic staff which may almost dictate that modules are taken as and when it is possible. And to do that modules have to be constructed which cover the ground as required for the accreditation regulations by the ILT. This presents no problem since the range of learning objectives which feature in most of the programmes referred to can be summarised and provided under such headings as:

- Delivering teaching and facilitating learning.
- Managing the assessment process.
- Curriculum evaluation and development.

Or as others which have appeared in the comments on previous programmes.

A large university adopted a direct approach to the professional development of its junior academic staff. Its information pamphlet begins interrogatively. 'What more might you want in your tutorial role?' You may want to:

> Learn more about the practice of teaching in higher education.
> Develop further your teaching abilities.
> Learn more of the theory of learning and teaching in higher education.
> Discuss your current teaching and new approaches with colleagues.
> Receive feedback and advice about developing and showing your teaching ability.

You may also want a qualification in teaching (and/or course design) in higher education.

And the pamphlet goes on to describe how all that can be accomplished.

As an approved SEDA course and one accredited to the ILT, all the outcomes and underpinning principles are consistent with those mentioned already. However, one distinguishing feature of this provision is that there are two courses offered at different levels hierarchically, where the content on the higher level course is an extension of the material of the first, moving up a conceptual notch. There is an AP(E)L route on offer for each of the two courses. Like many others, the compilation of a portfolio is the main source of evidence of achievement of the various aspects of the course. Unlike some others, there is an explicit requirement that participants make a written claim based on that evidence to have met all the requirements of the course. And assessment is based on that portfolio.

It is on completion of the second that a participant arrives at the SEDA Accredited Teacher Status, eligibility for membership of the ILT and a Postgraduate Certificate in Teaching and Learning in Higher Education which carries 60 academic credit points towards a Master's degree.

The different flavours and characteristics of such a range of courses, all of which have been treated on the same basis for accreditation by the ILT, supports its claims that in respecting the differences between institutions it is more interested in diversity than conformity, anxious to avoid unnecessary constraints, and sees itself more as an enabling institution rather than a regulatory one.

7 Towards individual membership

Given the response to the fast track opportunity which has led by September 2000 to a total membership of some 2,500 out of a total number of 130,000 academics, 1,800 of them part-time staff, not to speak of all the support staff which are eligible for membership in the system, there is a very long way to go.

Who comes next? it is likely that part of the next wave of applications for membership will come from those newly appointed academics and learning support staff, starting a career in higher education, or those who have taken up positions in higher education for the first time on the basis of their experience outside higher education. There may be others who embarked on an ILT accredited programme in one institution, succeeded in securing an appointment in another institution, and want to complete the necessary requirements for membership without loss of time or unnecessary duplication. But there are also likely to be some experienced academics who did not use the fast track and later for whatever reason seek membership, and for them the AP(E)L route will be far more attractive than any other mode so the AP(E)L side of the business may increase sharply.

For all of them the decision about which route, formal course or AP(E)L, to take will be influenced by a number of different factors. Some may feel they have insufficient experience to draw on to produce the necessary evidence out of their own heads and files under the five heads of responsibility. This may be simply because the roles they have had limit the range of experience to draw on. The set-piece programme may be best for them. Later they may decide that some element based on AP(E)L would help them along. Depending on the structure of the particular programme it may be possible to undertake some element through AP(E)L during the period of the course rather that declaring it at registration time. For others a mixture of 'taught course' and AP(E)L may be best. Indeed institutions may well incorporate that mixture into their own programme. Institutional rules differ. For example, by calling a programme a work-based learning route, and offering tutorial support to produce a portfolio for assessment on the taught route, staff can get all the available credits for the postgraduate certificate to square with the rule which says that the certificate cannot be completed by AP(E)L alone. Others may be daunted by hearsay evidence that producing a portfolio of evidence for AP(E)L is an exhausting and exacting business. Some may look at the relative time schedules of different approaches. But there are other factors which can impinge on what appears to be an academic judgement. Others again may prefer to take the opportunity for formal learning through following an ILT accredited programme because they like to find themselves in a group, studying with colleagues on a regular basis to the rather solitary business of reflecting on experience which is the hallmark of AP(E)L.

Having sorted out initially which pathway to take, those choosing the AP(E)L route will need to separate right at the beginning any prior learning which has been certificated in some way from experiential learning drawn from their experience and is uncertificated.

Whichever pathway looks most inviting the first step towards membership is to study carefully their institution's programme which has been accredited by the ILT. The programme document will lay out the modules in the programme, their specification, the nature of the evidence to be submitted, the assessment procedure involved and the general arrangements for advanced standing. That sorting out will clarify for a potential applicant for membership which of the requirements, if any, have been met already through courses taken previously as part of a postgraduate certificate, a CPD programme or a certificate or diploma taken for different reasons. That sorting out will also identify those modules and their requirements which have not been met through formal courses, but may well have been covered through experiential learning. Equipped with that knowledge of what has and what has not been accomplished through a combination of prior and experiential learning, what remains to be done will be self-evident.

There is a caveat, however. It can save much trouble later. When reviewing what may be offered as prior learning to be counted against an element in the institution's programme and then going on to experiential learning which may cover different modules in the programme, it is vital to ensure that no element of double counting comes in. It is very easy in some cases to get so involved in working out the experiential learning which may meet a course requirement that the fact that some prior learning has already covered the same element gets forgotten. This becomes self-evident when collating the evidence to support claim with either prior or experiential learning. The first will be in some form of a certificate. The second means producing evidence which has not been formally assessed before. This may be the design of a course plan, records of the preparation for and then the use of teaching and learning materials, examples and assessments of student work, and reflections on one's own professional performance, peer group observations if there are any, and personal attempts at an overall evaluation. That can represent a substantial undertaking. It is why it is so important to make sure at the beginning that there can be no danger of double counting between prior and experiential learning. There could easily be another complication. Where qualifications are not recognised by the ILT for equivalence like the PGCE or MEd there could be some difficulty in deciding the level and amount of credit to be awarded when read off against the modules in a programme. After checking over those possibilities in the course, the next decision is how to acquire the evidence necessary to meet the requirements of the outstanding modules. Will it be by formal study with a tutor as guide and mentor, or by private study which comes out in good time as experiential learning?

At this stage it is also as well to think through carefully about the Continuing Professional Development requirements for remaining in good standing with the ILT. Remaining in good standing will mean submitting evidence of CPD activities undertaken during the five-year period at the end of which memberships will be reviewed. This is well worth doing at this stage because coming to a decision about which route to take towards membership could easily produce ideas about the kind of CPD programme to pursue in the future.

Assuming that Route 2 is chosen, the next decision is whether it is to be AP(E)L applied to the institution's accredited programme or whether it is going to be a solo effort to meet the requirements set out in the five headings by extracting evidence of learning by systematic reflection on experience.

Whichever way that decision goes there are three sets of tasks to be tackled to be successful in Route 2: intellectual tasks, preparation tasks and submission tasks. The intellectual tasks subdivide into two; the distinction between descriptions of experience and identifying what has been learned from those experiences, and the difference between advocacy and judgement.

To distinguish between the description of an event or experience and an account of what was learned from that event or experience looks a pretty obvious business. In fact it is a teasing business. It is quite extra-ordinary how trained academics find this more difficult than they expect. In an attempt to effect the switch from description to an account of learning the tendency is to produce ever more refined descriptions. The blunt question – so what did you learn? – is the necessary corrective whether in an internal private conversation or with a tutor/advisor/ mentor.

Take an obvious example from the first of the five headings: teaching and support of learning. Any teacher claiming to be effective in promot-ing learning in students will have prepared the entire course/module/ unit with an eye on increasing the complexity of the material to be grasped as the course develops, with teaching aids to facilitate learning, whether overheads, videos, audio tape, artefacts, experiments or pro-grammes drawn down from the internet. It will have made sure that students are clear about the assessment procedures to be used, in relation to the syllabus description and the learning intentions which set out what the entire sequence is designed to help students learn. To make sure that the students understand what they are in for, all that will be printed and set out in attractively designed handouts. No one can claim not to know.

Now there is no doubt that a course which runs like that indicates a very thorough approach to the professionalism of teaching. But it all amounts to a description of activities. It is a list, and a very impressive list, too, which begins to get near the sort of evidence the ILT is looking for. But of itself that list of descriptions does not provide the requisite evidence to answer two fundamental questions: How effective was all that activity in meeting its declared purposes of promoting student learning? Where is the evidence that the tutor concerned has learned how to improve the promotion of student learning from the experience of teaching the course? There need to be clear statements setting out the claims to answering those two questions. And of course there has to be evidence to support the claims.

One way of answering the first question is by examining students' results. Again, that seems pretty obvious. But it is notoriously difficult to deduce anything more than the widest generalisations from them. Student evaluations are equally suspect, given the range of subjective variables which they are bound to contain. However, since it is the tutor rather than students themselves which are the prime concern of the ILT, perhaps trying to answer the second question may give hints about answers to the first.

There are several questions which the tutor can pose as an internal debate and analysis about the activities in the list of descriptions.

Were all the activities necessary and was the sequence in which they were used most helpful to the students? Despite the need for reinforcement to promote learning was there unnecessary duplication in using the full range of teaching aids. If there was, which activities should be dropped? Which activity drew out the most attentive, enthusiastic, purposeful response from students? Was the connection between the formal teaching, whether in didactic form or discussion, and the material in the teaching aids clear to the student? What about the increasing complexity of the material to be learned. Were the students aware of it? Did the tutor have a sense that that progression was being experienced by the students? Given the amount of time available was the content too great, too small or just about right. Probing questions like that will get near to being able to form a judgement about the overall effectiveness of the course in enabling students to grasp what the course was all about.

All that is a means of trying to work out what the tutor him/herself had learned from teaching the course. But where is the evidence of what had been learned? It has to be written down. It has to contain two parts; a claim stating what was learned, and the evidence to support the claim. Remembering is a peculiar business. Trying to summon up answers to all those self-interrogations after the course is over, is a very risky business. Hence a blow-by-blow recording is the proven way of working in this mode of learning. It means some sort of journal of notes scribbled down after each session which can serve as memory joggers when it comes to writing things down for submission to the ILT.

It is obvious then that if there is to be a systematic approach to producing evidence of successful teaching and learning it is no good leaving everything until the course has finished and hoping that what had been learned with supporting evidence could be summoned up easily. For these ILT purposes, as well as preparing for teaching the course, a tutor needs to prepare the style, scope and detail of the internal interrogations which will follow. It is equally obvious that in this way the course will be improved and hence the students' learning. And it goes without saying that this is part of the professionalism which ought to inform all teaching in higher education.

At this point it could well be that scrutinising student results in tests, essays, presentations and notes about the contributions of students during discussion will show some relationship between those results and the reflections about possible improvement to the course itself. In other words, through concentrating on self-performance, insights may come as to its effectiveness as a mean of promoting learning.

All that is the intellectual task of differentiating between description and reliable assessable evidence of learning. It is connected with the other intellectual task of separating advocacy from judgement. The point here is that anyone concerned with helping students to learn has a natural tendency in some cases to support a student's efforts, almost as an advocate for a whole range of very complicated reasons and motives. That view of a student's learning is necessarily different from anyone charged with the responsibility of making academic judgements about the level, range and general adequacy of that same student's learning as a submission for formal assessment in relation to a publicly recognised qualification. This possible conflict is likely to occur when a tutor attempts the internal interrogation referred to already. It is all too easy not to see the rose-tinted glasses worn. This is where evidence recorded at the time becomes so important. ILT applicants need to be aware of it. It is for this reason of course that the ILT gives a clear brief to referees and then separates carefully the supporting evidence which they supply and the evidence which comes from the applicant.

Turning to the preparation tasks, there is some overlap with the intellectual tasks. But going right back to the beginning, the first preparation task is to review the modules in a programme and select those with requirements which could be met through AP(E)L. And to repeat the point it is then vital to check that there is no question that those modules have been covered by any prior learning which may be included as evidence of learning. It is vital to avoid any possibility of double counting – covering the same area of learning with its evidence in two different ways and seeking to have it recognised twice, whereas it is in fact the same submission being offered in two different ways.

When it comes to the third set of tasks, the submission tasks, much of the necessary homework will have been done by working through systematically the intellectual tasks. Clarity and brevity are the watchwords; and the second can induce the first. Preparing statements of learning which constitute claims to have met the requirements for a particular module implies being very careful to avoid the trap of thinking that descriptions equal evidence of learning. Equally it means thinking through what actually constitutes evidence to support the claim. Hearsay will not pass muster. To be valid and reliable any evidence cited must be verifiable independently. As well as teaching handouts and overheads, there could be videos of some learning sessions, just as there could be comments by a colleague impressed into the role of observer and the tutor's own subsequent reflection on that particular occasion.

Even the most cursory glance at the five areas which need to be covered for a satisfactory application for membership shows up the problems of overlap and therefore of double counting.

- teaching and/ or supporting learning in higher education;
- contribution to the design and planning or learning activities and/or programmes of study;
- provision of feedback and assessment of students' learning;
- contribution to the development of effective learning environments and student support systems;
- reflection on personal practice in teaching and learning and work to improve the teaching process.

The same collection of evidence put forward to meeting the requirements of one of those areas listed above, could well be suitable as evidence put forward as meeting the requirements of another section of the course. There can be nothing wrong with that; it is in the best academic tradition of working on the assumption that looking at an object or considering a text from more than one perspective can yield different answers. For ILT purposes, it is essential to articulate clearly how any item of evidence relates to one of the five areas delineated.

Before anything can be submitted to the ILT for consideration material has to be organised in a coherent fashion. Collation in fact. However, the collation of claims with supporting evidence may not be as straightforward as it seems. For instance, assume that both learning claim and its supporting evidence has been sorted out for the first area listed above – teaching and learning in higher education – broadly along the lines indicated earlier, in the differentiation of description from statements of learning. Dealing with the second area above – contribution to the design and planning of learning activities and or programmes of study – seems simply an extension of the first area of responsibility – teaching and supporting learning. Which of course it is. But it is implying that all the factors which go to making teaching and support systems for learning effective need to be taken to a different level, and applied to a broader field altogether.

This level is essentially backroom planning whereas the first area of concern is essentially frontroom performance in classrooms or laboratories or design studios. It means deciding on the content of a course or module or unit, writing the learning intentions in using that material, so that its rationale is evident to both staff and students, and then figuring out what are the best means of helping students to work on the content so as to get as near as possible to grasping what is specified in the learning intentions. Inevitably this means thinking through the pedagogy in relation to the nature of the content of the course being planned. Ideally of course it should mean taking into consideration the probability of there being an assortment of preferred learning styles among any group of students. That would mean providing a variety of means of learning – the same material as in some of the very successful learning centres where students can choose between using visual, audio and textual styles of learning – or any combination of them all. A learning claim with supporting evidence should not be too difficult to draft, although it is likely to take more time than the previous topic.

As for dealing with student assessment and keeping them abreast of their progress, any tutor in higher education who does not meet that requirement and is unable to both describe what they do and comment on its effectiveness, has some thinking to do. For a surprising number of academics assessment stops at the traditional essay, and having to think about assessment can be a helpful jolt. This is important because the way students understand the assessment procedures and the way they are given and receive comments on this work goes a long way to connecting with the fourth area set out above. For instance, one of the most frustrating experiences for anyone who has completed and handed in a piece of work is to wait as the weeks go by without getting it back. After an inquiry or two as to when it will be returned, it all becomes a rather embarrassing business which sours relationship between that tutor and that student. And then when it is returned and there are only rather perfunctory comments on it, relationships move from bad to worse. Worse still, since that experience is certain to be broadcast among fellow students, it is almost bound to be the case that the tutor will have 'lost' the class often without realising it. There are other pressing duties. The internal alibi may be tight. But as a contribution to student's learning it is thoroughly negative. Better to publish a calendar of dates for submission and return; and even though there may be a long interval between them at least there is a framework for everyone to work within.

It is rather the same with timekeeping. Getting to a session on time – or better just before it – can seem a very trivial matter; but essentially it is a matter of treating students with respect. And they notice it.

It is not so easy to separate the fourth area of responsibility from the second. Planning a course of study in all its aspects inevitably can overlap with 'contributing to the creation of effective learning environments'. But conducive learning environments can take the form of both the purely cerebral and physical. Assuming that it is the physical aspects of creating effective learning environments which are concerned with the planning of courses, then this area is an opportunity to cite evidence of contributing to students' learning by paying close attention to where that learning takes place. Room decoration, colour and texture, furniture layout, floor covering, these are some of the things which go to creating an effective learning environment. All that may mean a fight with the Institution's resources or maintenance manager and it may well not be winnable. But the ILT requirement can be cited to support the argument. And although it all may sound rather banal compared with the cerebral side of planning for learning, in many cases it is just as important. Any teacher who has not noticed, felt, experienced the difference pleasing surroundings can make to students' learning has either been stuck in uncongenial accommodation or is strangely insensitive. There ought to be plenty of evidence to cite in making a claim to have met those requirements. What is sure, though, is that tutors can make a world of difference to the context they provide for learning by being polite, making it clear when and where they can be contacted and being appreciative of students' questions and comments.

'Reflection on personal practice in teaching and learning and work to improve the teaching process.' That is the last area where satisfactory evidence of accomplishment is required. It is a pity that the language fails to do justice to the nature of the topic; but unlike some overlaps mentioned earlier here the overlap is almost complete. One way or another all the preceding areas of responsibility imply that to be met there has to be some conscious reflection on day-to-day work with some sort of systematic self-evaluation of performance. This seeks to take that activity to a deeper level.

It follows from the ILT's commitment to flexibility that these requirements are not restricted to those who can meet them through having teaching as their primary responsibility. That has to mean that it is open to those with substantial administrative or organisational responsibilities to make claims to meet the requirements leading to membership. In reviewing those five areas of concern, it is obvious that many a head of department or faculty will be able to point to changes in procedure or deployment of staff or provision of staff development which are likely produce evidence of a different character from, say, novice teachers but relate directly to the particular topic. But just as for novice teachers, more senior staff will need to be able to make clear and concise statements of what has been learned in whatever its context, and produce evidence which relates directly to that claim and supports its validity.

Reflection is something of a buzz word in staff development. It is merely a dolled-up version of thinking about what you are doing and taking steps to try to prove it. That is implied in every particular of the ILT requirements for membership. But in many ways that is just putting a public label on what so many academics do as a matter of course; think about what they are doing. New ideas can come from anywhere about presentation. Content may need reviewing if too many students seem to fail to grasp it. Worries can nag away about how to wean students from wanting information to pass examinations and tease them into proper study of a subject; student reflection indeed. What the ILT membership requirements do is to put greater emphasis on exploiting academics' own reflection so that it becomes a conscious means of learning; what works, what does not, and in any case how to improve the service for promoting students' learning.

8 Fast track to membership

Under the title of Initial Entry for experienced staff the ILT document laid out a different route towards membership that had been devised for experienced practitioners. The 'fast track'. This was because:

> it is essential for the success of the ILT that its membership includes both experienced and new staff and that experienced staff in particular are attracted into membership at an early stage.

Equally, the ILT must be able to show that all routes to membership require the same level of attainment. All members will also be expected to undertake Continuing Professional Development (CPD) in the five broad areas of:

- teaching and support of learning;
- contribution to the design and planning of learning activities;
- assessment giving feedback to students;
- developing effective learning environments and student learning support systems;
- reflective practice and personal development.

In an attempt to reach those experienced staff, until September 2001, in other words two years from its beginning, the ILT has devised a 'fast track'. It will accept into membership via this route staff who 'have the equivalent of three years' full-time experience of teaching or learning support in HE, . . . part-time staff and those whose roles include limited responsibility for teaching or learning support are encouraged to apply through this route if they have the equivalent of three years' full-time experience'.

Procedurally this fast track route involves individuals completing forms supplied by the ILT which come in two parts. The first is to record all the usual personal and professional details which an organisation requires; a form of tabulated, abbreviated CV. The second is the serious section where applicants have to summarise their claims to have met requirements in the five areas in the criteria for membership. For each topic there is a box provided for the response which is limited to 500 words as maximum. At the top of each box there is a guidance note. For example, for Teaching and Support of Learning, the guidance note reads:

> Please indicate the range of teaching and learning support activities in which you are involved. Give examples of successful activities or techniques you use and comment on how you came to use them and why you think they are successful. Include the proportion of time spent teaching/support learning, subjects and level taught, methods adopted and any special responsibilities you carry (such as Course, Programme or Subject leadership, or Head of Learning Support Unit).

At one level that briefing note looks as if it is asking for a list of activities and responsibilities. That is most certainly not the case. Lists are not what are required. What those 500 words are looking for are reflections on whatever activities and responsibilities may be adduced, some indication as to what has been learned from them along the way and what evidence there is to prove that such learning has taken place as well as that of students.

This becomes clear when reviewing the comparable briefing note for accreditors. These are experienced academics recruited by the ILT to assess and make recommendations about applications for membership under the fast track facility. The accreditors' guidance notes for that same first box on Teaching and Support for Learning reads:

> Please comment on whether the range of teaching and learning support activities given is appropriate for the educational context (appropriateness to subject, level, intended learning outcomes and the student profile). Please indicate whether you found evidence of a rationale for choosing activities and techniques used and how they relate to developing the learners' understanding of the subject.

Similar notes head each of the following five boxes: contribution to the design and planning of learning activities; assessment and giving feedback to students; developing effective learning environments and student learning support systems; reflective practice and personal development; and other information. And of course for each there is a parallel briefing note for accreditors: but not until the final box is reached dealing with reflective practice and personal development does the reflective and learning elements implied by each briefing note become explicit.

These briefing notes are being revised but it is a pity that from the beginning this fast track procedure did not put greater emphasis on what tutors have learned from the experience of teaching and how they reflected upon it. That way alone can lead to considered improvement in practice. That is the central purpose of the ILT. So it rather looks as if its anxiety to secure substantial numbers of members in its first period of operation has led to somewhat hasty provision.

A vital part of this Part 2 of the application for membership by experienced staff concerns the naming of two referees. They must have recent and direct knowledge of the work of the applicant and what they are expected to do. They have to read the submission the applicant has prepared for submission to the ILT, corroborate the evidence cited and authenticate it by signing it. The ILT makes it explicit that this is a different kind of refereeing:

> This is a different kind of reference from one that is normally required for promotion or appointment as we are looking for evidence of commitment to teaching and/of supporting learning rather than general academic achievement.

Once all that documentation has arrived at the ILT, everything is handed over to accreditors. These are experienced academics who applied for appointment as accreditors and have been trained and recruited for this purpose. Accreditors work in pairs. Separately each member of a pair reads up to eight applications in a day, so that those eight applications have been double marked as either Accept or Refer. Those applications are then handed to another pair of accreditors, acting as moderators of the decisions reached by the first pair. Referrals are discussed and if agreements cannot be reached by three of the four accreditors then at a third layer of assessment a final decision is taken. Recommendations from the accreditors then go to the Accreditation Committee. Referrals are dealt with by tactful letters from the Institute itself giving the reasons for referral and giving advice on those areas which need strengthening. ILT officers and staff have no role in the accreditation. They are simply the administrative support force to keep things moving smoothly. From start to finish the ILT has committed itself to getting through all the work in not more than twelve weeks.

As a procedure this seems rigorous on paper. The working in pairs means that in all four accreditors review each application and have to record Accept/Refer on each. If they cannot agree about a particular application it gets referred and all four then meet. If they cannot agree about an application it gets referred to a third level of accreditation where the final decision is taken.

Unfortunately, the fast track has had a baleful effect on some institutions and therefore has come in for some heavy criticism. This is hardly surprising because some institutions found that some academics who opted for the fast track were the very same colleagues who previously had followed the well-established staff development courses which the institution had been running for its staff for many years. So it seemed that the ILT was undermining well-established courses in individual universities leading to internally devised Certificates of Diplomas in HE teaching. Many of these courses represent a large investment of staff time in planning and providing such courses, using standard HE assessment procedures, including external examiners. To find all this threatened by a newcomer to the business is frustrating and for some damaging. This undermining was because from all appearances the fast track offered experienced staff a way of acquiring a HE teaching qualification with a great deal less effort than signing up for a year long course.

Also it is claimed that the fast track undermines the careful insistence on standards for an AP(E)L route in earlier documents. Indeed some institutions with good experience of working with AP(E)L for students say that the ILT's procedure for academics is less rigorous than that applied to students.

For individuals, opinions are divided about this way of meeting the commitment to find routes to membership for experienced academics. Some academic staff responsible for staff development in their own institutions gave seminars on how to deal with the requirements of the fast track. Some observe that being clever people, when advised to include indications of reflection in their 500 word answers, they are perfectly capable of doing so despite having reflected little on their own teaching over the years. The question then is whether or not these people should be members of the ILT. Some very experienced practitioners of AP(E)L say that the fast track is neither one thing nor another. Being sceptical of the assessment procedure makes them chary of anything which is not a full-blown portfolio. At the other extreme these people wonder whether it would have been better to admit anyone who applied and then rely on the Continuing Professional Development (CPD) to sort things out later. That is and was utterly impracticable and inappropriate, so the fast track stands in these people's eyes as a cover-up for admitting to membership as many as possible as fast as possible. In other words, it is not only fast, but cheap and nasty. References may be by chums and not worth the paper on which they are written.

For example, one senior head of department contrasted the very hard work required to become a member or a fellow of professional institutions with that of seeking membership of the ILT through the fast track. The claim was that this was an inadequate way of seeking evidence of true professionalism. This was balanced by the recognition that the requirement to reflect on practice was a very constructive line to take because the normal course of day-to-day events tended to crowd out that very important aspect of teaching in higher education.

Conversely, some who have attempted to cope with the topics in 500 words – and accreditors reject pieces which are obviously longer than that – find that it is a rigorous requirement for disciplined thought and expression. Some hardened sceptics admit to finding that the task really does prompt rigorous reflection.

Obviously there is a dispute about how far that criticism is justified, that the ILT has debased the currency, not only of membership but of AP(E)L. From the applicants' point of view there is no doubt that the intellectual demands of summarising succinctly in 500 words material to satisfy each of the five topics noted already are considerable. It might be assumed that those versed in the language and practice of staff development would have an advantage over lecturers in particular disciplines. This turns out to be no means the case in many instances. An accreditor made the point that sometimes academics who thought and wrote from outside the territory of education aficionados were sometimes the more convincing and thoughtful than, say, education experts, as they tried to give an account of what they had learned from their own experience. This is a very important revelation. It could suggest even that the ILT had got it right. If AP(E)L works like that for subject experts then it is being supported rather then undermined as was first feared.

It is also important for a different reason. The fast track is bound to be acting as sort of a dummy run for the full-scale operation of the ILT when the fast track is over and done with. If the accumulated experience of those academics who have submitted applications under the fast track arrangements and the experience of those academics acting as accreditors for individual submissions suggests that the approach used to AP(E)L is valid and reliable, then the ILT will be a great deal more secure in its procedures for individual membership than at the outset of their activities.

The rubrics for each of the sections on the fast track application are being revised so that greater emphasis is given to what has been learned from the activities described rather than an account of activities themselves. Despite being very clever, not all academics take easily to the notion of careful reflection on what they actually do, day-by-day. But that is the central requirement for the fast track, and so stronger pointers are needed to encourage systematic reflection. Inevitably some will become members just through cleverness of expediency so that the validity of the fast track will depend on the rigour of the CPD which follows on.

Jumping forward to 2001 and leaving the fast track behind, there are accredited courses and accredited routes or pathways towards membership. A question is how far the experience of the fast track affects ILT as a whole. For the ILT a course includes taught elements which go to meet the requirements of the five areas. A route or pathway is a set of activities that enable staff to accumulate evidence that they have met the requirements for membership. However, a pathway need not include taught courses but should involve formal evaluation of the evidence against ILT requirements. Both, though, need to be able to demonstrate that applicants have a sound understanding of the core knowledge and an adherence to professional values.

For the ILT core knowledge is:

• the subject material that they will be teaching;
• appropriate methods for teaching and learning in the subject area and at the level of the academic programme;
• models of how students learn, both generically and in their subject;
• the use of learning technologies appropriate to the context in which they teach;
• methods for monitoring and evaluating their own teaching;
• the implications of quality assurance for practice.

Professional values are cited as:

• a commitment to scholarship in teaching, both generally and within their own discipline;
• respect for individual learners and their development and empowerment;

- a commitment to the development of learning communities, including students, teachers and all those engaged in learning support;
- a commitment to encouraging participation in higher education and to equality of educational opportunity;
- a commitment to continued reflection and evaluation and consequent improvement of their own practice.

In each case the usual components of quality assurance systems apply. There need to be:

- procedures for ensuring the quality of the course involving all involved in its delivery;
- procedures for monitoring, review and evaluation of the course leading to action and change;
- the involvement of the participants in monitoring and evaluation of the course;
- involvement of external people in programme review.

Equally, of course, there can be no risk of differential standards between the different routes for membership, fast track included. To this end institutions applying for accreditation of any kind will have their arrangements scrutinised by a visiting panel of accreditors. They will have read all the documentation beforehand, which dealt with staffing and resources, as well as the course documents themselves, spent a day in the institution, and drafted a report which goes to the institution for factual checking. After all that, the panel then makes a recommendation to the Accreditation Committee.

This detail of itself which the ILT put into public circulation in August 1999 makes it clear that the entire enterprise is based on peer review. From government's hands-off approach, through the membership criteria and the routes towards membership to the accreditation procedure itself, it is clear that the ILT's view of a professional body puts it on a par with other professional bodies. It is governed by its members. This is enshrined in its constitution as a membership organisation, where it is members who are in charge, and therefore answerable to their own peers in institutions. How successful it is is bound to be influenced by the views throughout higher education about the status of the ILT.

In line with the requirements of other professional bodies, the ILT is not content to receive people into membership and leave it at that. To remain in good standing members are required to produce evidence of participation in some form of Continuing Professional Development. How far there is willingness of individuals as members to engage in CPD is bound to be influenced by experiences of the fast track. And that is the topic for the next chapter.

9   Towards a scholarship of teaching: continuing professional development

Continuing Professional Development (CPD) has to be a requirement for membership of the ILT. But it lands it in the middle of tensions which exist and have been increasing between regulatory bodies and institutions which then impinge on individuals and through them to the membership organisations they may belong to. The way it positions itself within those tensions is likely to have a defining influence on its status and standing in higher education as a whole.

Without a requirement for members to undertake CPD as a condition for remaining in good standing, it is impossible to see how the ILT can even begin to realise the key part of the Dearing recommendation; membership to be established as 'normal' for academics in higher education. This expectation is something new. It may seem far-fetched, and probably unrealisable but that is the context for teachers in higher education in the twenty-first century. And whichever way it is looked at, it seems that AP(E)L will be a significant contributor to these overall intentions.

That may be the context, but the way the ILT handles CPD will be a powerful influence on the way it is regarded in the academic community. And the way it pays attention to the learning and teaching in specialist disciplines is likely to be the key to that.

Whatever it is, though, it is not straightforward. CPD can be expressed through the customary differentiation between academic staff learning, student learning and organisation learning. Scholarly approaches can be taken to the topics of professional development, personal development, the complicated question of appraisal and the associated topic of mentoring. Similarly teaching and learning styles, curriculum and curriculum design, student support, resources and libraries and the hidden curriculum can all be tackled at a scholarly level. So can management structures, power relationships, and all the elements which go to make up how an institution uses its facilities to promote whatever it perceives as its overriding purpose. All that is a rich arena for scholarly study. There are no limits to what individual academics may chose to do for their CPD. The ILT has to find some way of accommodating such an almost limitless range of activity as the CPD which keeps an individual's membership in good standing.

Those intentions contrast sharply with the earlier standing of in-service work for teachers. For a long time CPD had a bad name with school teachers. In the United States where for teachers CPD had been often a condition of employment, frequently it was no more than going through the motions of following courses, getting them listed on some official record, almost irrespective of whether the course topic related to their current responsibilities as teachers or not. In this country there was a tendency to be a bit sniffy about the idea that serving professionals needed to take special means to do the job they were doing.

For school teachers in Britain that changed as a proposition when the James Report on Teaching Training in 1971 contained a proposal for the establishment of Professional Tutors in Schools with regional arrangements to cover all the country to support the development of teachers. There had been plenty of in-service provision, as it was then called, before the James Report. But after its publication for Local Education Authorities, teachers' unions, colleges of education and universities provision of in-service moved up the priority order, often encouraged to do so by government through a series of financial support mechanism. Universities and much of higher education then took to providing their own versions of CPD as the need became more evident that the changing composition of the student body meant thinking afresh about how best to serve them. And there was a proliferation of postgraduate certificates, diplomas and Master's degrees. All this despite the fact that the James proposals almost predictably disappeared down the black hole of 'cannot be afforded'.

Doctors, lawyers and the medical profession have for a long time had some provision for further development, if for no other reason than to keep abreast with the latest techniques in physicians' treatment of patients and surgical practice. Dramatic advances such as open heart surgery and the ever more sophisticated diagnosis of disease underlines that need for CPD which then becomes a heated element in the contentious issue of self-regulation or external regulation as reports of incompetency multiply.

Under the strong leadership of the English Nation Board (ENB) and the United Kingdom Central Council (UKCC) for the registration of nurses and midwives, CPD for nurses has not only increased in volume but under pressure from reforms which change the role of many nurses it has been absolutely essential. As a result, the ILT has offered immediate application for membership from registered nurses, midwives and health visitors who qualified with the UK Central Council and who have a UKCC recorded teaching qualification, on the grounds that they can play a fuller role in higher education and help to shape the future of professional self-regulation.

In passing, two points are worth remarking. The ENB was among the first, if not *the* first professional body to grasp the possibilities offered to its members by AP(E)L and invested heavily in devising procedures to use it. So tacitly that decision by the ILT is acknowledging over a wider field than its own the validity and reliability of AP(E)L for professional and academic recognition. And then that decision is an indication of a different kind of tension for the ILT; how to obtain members while ensuring that, as the ILT itself puts it, 'Equally it must be able to show that all routes to membership require the same level of achievement'. Some hold the view that admitting nurses on those criteria is cheapening the currency of membership. Others would claim that the UKCC's requirements are as tough if not tougher than those for the fast track.

Other professions too show the same drive for professionalism: accountancy, the law, and engineering for example. In every sphere, new legisation, new procedures, new techniques require professionals to be keeping up-to-date constantly. The huge spread and increase in the provision of Master's degrees in Business Administration – MBAs – is but another indication of the need felt by business, industry and commerce to have a steady flow of employees who are as up-to-date as possible with whatever it takes to boost productivity and profit.

But behind all these developments in providing further learning for people in the professions at a postgraduate level lies the general tendency for there to be increasing regulation. For a whole range of extremely complicated reasons during the period since the end of the second world war there has been a steady withdrawal of trust from almost every institution which can be thought of. Medicine, the law, teachers at every level from schools to higher education, local authorities, the police, sections of the general public no longer trust them. Both the monarchy and the BBC get drawn into public controversies which used to be handled in private. And of course the politicians themselves are regarded with some cynicism. A better educated population with a consistently rising standard of living is better informed than previous generations and very naturally is prone to asking tricky questions. It is less deferential.

So governments under pressure to justify levels of taxation seek means of demonstrating that the tax payers' money is being well spent. Where government has a direct stake financially, whether it be local authorities, schools and higher education, the NHS, it intervenes directly, inventing additional ways of scrutinising what actually goes on and using financial and sometimes legal means of doing so. Where it cannot intervene directly, it tries to do so indirectly through influence and inevitably there are disputes. Current debates about the way police inquiries are conducted into allegations of malpractice are a case in point. So are the pressures being brought to bear on the General Medical Council to tighten and toughen its procedures for dealing with complaints about the professional performance of individual doctors. By appointing regulators for public services under a privatised system – gas, electricity, communications, transport, and so on – government does what it can to meet the same issues of finding ways of ensuring high professional standards in those offering the service.

Whilst the intention is undoubtedly correct, the difficulty lies in collecting and making public evidence which gives reliable statements about the standards of service being achieved. On all sides there are attempts to make every aspect of a professional's performance transparent and measurable so that anyone can understand the evidence made public and can make their own judgements about its quality. There are league tables galore, but there are too many variables to make them more than general statements and indicative of trends.

Something of the same drive is at work in other forms of employment. With an eye on the growing tendency among the general public to lodge complaints, some building sites display notices such as 'Considerate Construction' adding that the company adheres to a code of practice and that any complaints should be addressed to the manager whose name is given on the notice. Parks sometimes carry notices too issued by a local authority's Leisure and Community Service, announcing that complaints should be addressed to the Parks Department.

All of this finds its way into the consciousness of politicians as they tend their weekend surgeries in their constituencies. It finds its way into election manifestos in order to justify public expenditure; it finds its way into politicians' thinking and so a party forming a government tends to have a commitment to use regulations to maintain standards and will urge professions to keep themselves up-to-date through CPD.

This takes us to the Dearing Committee. It was the turn of higher education to get caught up further in government supported national programmes for improvement. To this end the Dearing Committee made its recommendation for the creation of the ILT. How far that was a deliberate ploy to resist some of the more questionable attempts of government to control quality in every conceivable public activity it is difficult to judge. But that recommendation has to be seen against the existence of OFSTED, the inspectorial body which has a very mixed press about its performance with schools and has an indifferent standing within higher education, and alongside the Quality Assurance Agency (QAA) which replaced the Higher Education Quality Council in 1994.

Whatever the true provenance of the ILT, to be effective any regulation in the professions needs a partner. It is called CPD. Regulation needs to have an accessible instrument for improvements where they are considered to be desirable and practicable. Just as the CVCP's initiative in establishing UCoSDA was in response to what it was anticipated that government might try to do if no initiative was taken, so the Dearing Committee's recommendation about CPD in relation to quality needs to be seen in the context of the QAA which by then was raising questions about quality and standards and making recommendations as a regulator. That is part of its job, to make pronouncements on standards; and in the present climate almost inevitably about the need to improve them, whether pronouncements were well founded or not. CPD therefore had to appear to be a viable way of attempting to reach higher standards. The Institute of Learning and Teaching is a CPD facility in the first instance for membership of the ILT. But then in line with professional membership organisations generally to remain in good standing there needs to be an obligation to stay up-to-date by additional professional development.

It is this question of CPD requirements to remain in good standing which so far has had no public pronouncement. In view of the minefield of reactions to whatever is eventually pronounced this is understandable even though it is unfortunate. In the first Booth consultation the proposed commitment was clear:

> Membership of a professional body normally carries with it an obligation to 'remain on good standing' to maintain the level of one's professional expertise and regularly update one's knowledge. Thus if it wishes to parallel the activities of other professional bodies, the Institute will need to establish: guidelines for a regular commitment to continuing professional development (CPD) for all its categories of membershipl; procedures for verifying these activities in terms of demonstrable outcomes achieved.
>
> (A4.1)

It went on to suggest that that might involve academics in between five and eight days' study time a year (A4.2).

In its recommendations the final report from the Booth Committee said of CPD:

> that the CPD commitment should be broadly defined as one based on action research, reflective practice and observation of teaching.

The Executive Summary of the CVCP's Report in the summer of 1998 set out its view of the purposes of an ILT as to:

> Enhance the recognition of teaching in higher education. Maintain and improve the quality of learning and teaching in higher education. Set standards of good professional practice that its members and in due course all those with teaching and learning responsibilities in higher education might follow.

It includes this as one of the key activities of the ILT:

> collect, analyse and disseminate existing research on teaching and learning practice.

(para 5)

In the full Report this was expanded:

> The development arm should focus on existing research and practice in teaching and learning by collecting existing data on teaching and learning practice; conducting a meta-analysis of the data; disseminating good practice to members through publication, conferences and the accreditation framework.

The first document issued by the ILT itself in October 1998 crossed the t's on that as:

> collection, analysis and dissemination of existing research on teaching and learning practice in accessible formats for use within the academic community.

The addition of those words 'for use within the academic community' could be taken as a pathetic attempt to claim ownership for something already decided, but it can also be seen as a deliberate piece of labelling to ensure that research should stay close to day-to-day concerns of ordinary teachers in higher education.

The Report from the Research and Development Working Group took this further. It insisted that research and development should be integral to the ILT's work so as to inform:

> both the development of its national accreditation purpose and the stimulation of innovation in its broadest sense.

In doing so it rested its case on passages from the Dearing Report:

> Placing higher education teaching on a more professional basis requires a strong foundation of theoretical and practical research into learning and teaching processes (8.64). It is especially important that research outcomes are used to inform policy and practice (and stimulate innovation) in learning and teaching (8.68). There is no place at present where such a body of knowledge can develop (8.64).

The Working Group went on to cite some principles which it thought ought to be followed in this enterprise. The ILT's role in CPD for its members should be to ensure that provision was:

- applied;
- directed by agenda provided by its constituencies;
- enabling;
- collaborative;
- exemplary;
- neutral;
- world class.

The unhappily instrumental and greatly unpopular consultation which the ILT issued in February 1999 had a section entitled 'The character of CPD activities'. It took the thinking a little further by usefully setting down the obvious, that evidence of CPD could be drawn from:

- professional work-based activities;
- personal activities outside work;
- courses, seminars, conferences and training events;
- self-directed and informal learning.

It produced the figure of 40 hours a year for an academic to accomplish the required amount of CPD, without explanation or justification. It listed every possible source of documentary and other evidence to support the claim that CPD requirements had been met. But then it tended to spoil things as the unfortunately instrumental flavour crept into the paragraph on Evaluating and Monitoring Professional Development Records. Assessors would judge the sufficiency, currency and match (of CPD records) to the national outcomes. As part of its accrediting and monitoring processes the ILT would require institutions to demonstrate their robust quality assurance procedures for verifying CPD for re-registration and the upgrading of membership categories. And *ex-cathedra* judgements would be issued from time to time by an ILT appointed accreditor. God was not invoked. Had He been so, most of higher education would have been declared as heretics.

Like most of this unattributed 1999 document, much of this was thrown out as a result of consultations with institutions. Those responses claimed that 40 hours was unrealistic. It was hardly necessary to say why. Any attempt to define CPD by hours is naive. Reflection on and modification of practice which are at the heart of improving teaching bear no relation to the number of hours spent in conferences, courses or anything else. Five years not three was the re-registration period. The guidelines were not acceptable. Procedurally the threat of too much bureaucracy was real and in any case monitoring was more the responsibility of individuals and their institutions. And for the suspicious, there was another whiff of attempts to centralise. In the light of all that which preceded the beginning of activities by the ILT it is no small wonder that it has been cautiously exploring the overall question of CPD.

All the approaches about CPD recommended through the various consultative stages of establishing the ILT could be seen according to a fivefold division as propounded in a 2000 paper commissioned by the Qualifications and Curriculum Authority (QCA); Standards and Vocational Qualifications in Continuing Professional Development (CPD). It talks about career development, improving and maintaining the quality of practice, expanding one's domain of competence, facilitating changes in practice and quality assurance for users and public. None of that is unusual. It begs the question of whether or not such items are to be required and enforced, and if so by whom, on what grounds, under whose authority.

It is the notion of expanding one's domain of competence as an element to CPD for teachers in higher education that is an interestingly suggestive way of thinking about it. The paper cites three aspects to this. There is the narrowing and deepening range of activities for some specialist purpose. There is the broadening of expertise from its present base. And there is the development of an organisational role in management. Put together those three elements seem to comprehend the possible range of content for the CPD which is appropriate to the ILT although the paper concerned all the professions, and made no mention of the ILT.

There are two vital aspects of CPD to be determined: definition, which means content, and verification. To be effective any CPD programme must take its cue from existing practice – where participating professionals actually are, as opposed to where someone else thinks they ought to be, and quite deliberately must move the discourse beyond it towards improving practice, but in a way which is seen by the professionals as practicable and affordable. If it can be both enjoyable and personally satisfying then the CPD has done its job. Verification lies somewhere along the line between over and under specification. Over specific verification is bound to imply constraints on what counts as CPD. For higher education that is inappropriate and had already been rejected. Under specification implies a sloppiness which is equally inappropriate. A balance requires some means of confirming that a given professional has continued to think about what he or she is doing, whether through keeping up-to-date in a subject or making a better job of managing or presenting or any aspect of an academic's work, in ways which are relevant to the responsibilities to be discharged.

Beyond saying that activities should promote improved practice, there is little indication in any of the papers of what CPD means in practice. The Booth Committee's view was:

> that the CPD commitment should be broadly defined as one based on action research, reflective practice and observation of teaching.

The Working Party said that CPD could be composed of any of the following:

- professional work-based activities;
- personal activities outside work;
- courses, seminars, conferences and training events;
- self-directed and informal learning.

That is a pretty obvious list and unimaginative. For example, neither in the list nor in any subsequent comment is there any reference to peer group mentoring, unless of course that is thought to be part of professional work-based activities. The trouble is that so far for CPD most attention tends to focus on courses, particularly postgraduate qualifications, seminars, conferences and training events. They are easy to log and record. But most cannot be said to be filled with imagination. The value of courses for professionals is in direct relation to the amount of genuinely new knowledge and skill the course provides which can be appreciated because it relates to day-to-day practice. This can be the case in those disciplines which are developing so fast – electronic communication, micro-biology, the study of the brain and so on. But it is far harder to devise courses in the theory and practice of education which answer that requirement. Similarly with seminars. Where there is a shared sense of inquiry, with thoughtful contributions so that one person's opinion becomes a trigger for another's thinking afresh or seeing something in a different way then seminars are fine. But all too often unskilled leadership and without a clearly stated purpose, seminars can easily deteriorate into general discussion which is interesting in itself but in no sense is exploring something new. It is the same with training events. They are effective when the participants are sure that they have something to gain from it. For example, training sessions are most certainly effective on how to help colleagues make submissions for membership of the ILT under the fast track procedure. From all accounts these have been more popular than any other staff development event.

The obvious exceptions to all this are the activities of the various specialist subject associations and professional bodies. Any discipline which features in a higher education curriculum somewhere is likely to have its own newsletter or periodical, its own networks, its own programme of meetings and conferences. All of this constitutes CPD of one kind or another.

At other times in these documents the phrase 'instances of good practice' appears. That is a clause inserted routinely in submissions for grant aid, and everyone knows that it is an extremely slippery concept. What is good practice for one institution is not necessarily good practice in another, nor for one individual and therefore for others. And a good thing, too, many would say. Diversity of style and approach is too precious to put at risk through any attempts at uniformity. Usually there are too many variables to take into account to run that risk. But more than that there is the simple question of how one person can be persuaded to take note of another's good practice.

That is the trouble with the third activity listed above – 'disseminating good practice to members through publication, conferences and the accreditation framework'. Take any instance of good practice developed by an individual or a group within an institution. Other colleagues cannot be compelled to take note of it. Nor can they be compelled to attend seminars. Writing snappy descriptions and putting them into circulation is essentially a hit and miss affair with responses coming from people who most likely are thinking about their professional practice anyhow. If dissemination within an institution is as difficult as that, and it is, then trying to think of text as the medium for spreading information about good practice nationally is flawed from the beginning. And it is no good relying on emails, the internet and the whole range of telecommunications facility to do the job. No matter how excellent the wording, the likelihood is that not many will read it. It has to compete for time and attention with extremely busy people who have all manner of documents to read and returns to make which command their time because they cannot be gainsaid. So by and large, words, however used, are unlikely to be a very successful means of dissemination.

To a large extent this is not so markedly the case for individual disciplines as it is for educational matters of learning and teaching. That may be a sad comment on the standing of education but it is indicative of the issue which the Dearing Committee faced and which runs through all the consultations up to the establishment of the ILT itself. Enhancing the status of teaching in higher education was, after all, one of its purposes.

But education tends to be a poor relation. However good some of its research it tends to get sneered at, and not always by people who know what they are talking about. So while it is good that Dearing related the recommendation for the ILT to enhancing the status of teachers in higher education, most academics do not see that lift in status coming from CPD in 'education'.

Part of the problem is the way that over the years heavy emphasis has been put on research, now essentially for funding purposes, at the expense of all the other professional responsibilities that a higher education carries with it. There is no need to rehearse the issues at length here. Questions of individual rewards and of institutional funding lie at the heart of the argument. And they will do so until learning and teaching get lifted up the reputation ladder. The ILT and all the staff developers have an uphill task.

There is a solution. Ernest Boyer pointed to it. As Head of the Carnegie Foundation for the Advancement of Teaching some time ago he drew on his book, *Scholarship Reconsidered: Priorities of the Professoriate 1990*, when he gave a lecture in the Royal Society on education. He spent a significant part of his time addressing the skewing of higher education through what he called the 'publish and get granted' culture. He argued that 'Research and publication have become the primary means by which most professors achieve academic status, yet many academics are drawn to the profession precisely because of their love for teaching and service.' He claimed that 'This has devalued teaching and on many campuses it is a culture that restricts creativity rather than sustains it.'

To correct this imbalance between teaching and research he called for a broader way of looking at scholarship. He identified four different but overlapping categories. He suggested that there was a Scholarship of Discovery Research; a Scholarship of Integration, including the writing of textbooks; a Scholarship of Service, including the practical application of knowledge which for him included service in the community; and a Scholarship of Teaching. So his solution was to get recognition for the Scholarship of Teaching as an academic activity in its own right, alongside other forms of academic scholarship some of which move into the pure research bracket.

There is more in that than might appear at first reading. Put together Boyer's Scholarship of Service and his Scholarship of Teaching and there is a potent prescription for extending the role of teaching. Implicitly it is challenging any narrow definition of teaching. If the Scholarship of Integration is added, then the terrain for teaching is extended again. Related to his thesis that the current relationship between research and teaching 'is a culture that restricts creativity rather than sustains it', that extension is just what he was talking about with the unspoken warning that it was ignored at great peril.

Years before Dearing, that is almost on cue for the Institute of Learning and Teaching. It certainly points to the role it is being invited to assume. Its target has to become the promotion of the Scholarship of Teaching. And it connects directly with the questions about CPD. Boyer was careful to insist that it was an institutional responsibility to work out what this meant for its own academics. That is in line with the posture adopted by the ILT in relation to institutional autonomy. But it moves no nearer to setting out what are the most effective forms of CPD. Nor of its content. What would Scholarship of Learning and Teaching look like if it were put down on paper?

With the exception of where outright didactic approaches are desirable, there seem to be two guiding principles for providing CPD in learning and teaching. One is that seeing and feeling through experience is the most effective mode for most people. The other is that the source of CPD is irrelevant provided that what has been learned is recorded appropriately.

For 160 academics and administrators the most effective CPD they ever experienced was spending a week on a Study Tour to the USA to get first-hand knowledge of how AP(E)L was being used in the programmes of community colleges and four-year universities up and down the East coast of America. More than that they learned a great deal about the flexibililty it was possible to create in institutional practices where there was a mind to do so. The reasons they were so effective were perfectly obvious. Take a small group of four or five people from different institutions for a week, expose them to the same experiences which are then experienced through the lens of their own institution while translating them mentally into possibilities back home and a never-ending running seminar is the result. In the bars, in airports, while travelling and over evening meals the talking never stopped. Comments from participants ranged from 'a uniquely success-ful mode of professional staff development' through 'variously inform, modify, improve or confirm professional practice', to 'exert a catalytic influence on curricula developments'. Some even said: 'It changed my life' and the most important thing that had happened to them profes-sionally (*Learners All – Worldwide*: 1997 Learning from Experience Trust). Reflection on the experiences equalled learning. What more could be asked? What can be asked but not answered is whether the most important learning occurred during visits, during the myriad of unscripted conversations, from chance remarks with American hosts, or from private thoughts in bed, bathroom or bar.

In some ways this can be presented as an expensive luxurious way to think of CPD. In fact it was not so. Averaging something like £1,500 for the week with everything paid – flights, accommodation, meals, internal transport – it was less than for an institution paying the fees for many a postgraduate course. And if being away for five working days seems difficult to fit in, comparisons with all the other reasons that those same academics were away from their own institutions but engaged on what is essentially higher education work, it is all quite manageable. In other words Study Tours were not only relatively cheap. They were far more effective that many other forms of CPD.

The entire Study Tours programme rested on the assumption that the week following a broadly based programme of visits arranged to meet the interests of the members of the group, with occasional intervention by the leader when it appeared that inquiries were going up a cul-de-sac, was a great deal better than trying to plan everything in advance.

In other words, people took from the shared experience whatever it was that was appropriate for them. No one tried to prescribe that for them. They were engaged in independent study. Mentoring was at hand. The motivation was strong. In most ways the learning acquired was unquantifiable. The success story of the Study Tours programme means that as a concept it is a powerful version of CPD.

This begins to sound like scholarship. Scholars do not have their topics, scope, methods or timescale prescribed for them. They may seek help and advice on aspects of their study. But they are not necessarily engaged in research as it is commonly understood. Their study is to help them master a topic. They take their time. They want to think about it. That is scholarship.

It can be expressed in several different ways, ways which tally with the predilections of different individuals. There is the professional in a particular discipline or professional area who takes the trouble to remain up-to-date with the latest research developments. There are professionals who read methodically the contributions in journals, books and articles which focus on the techniques and approaches to learning and teaching in a particular discipline. There are other professionals who make those contributions themselves. And others still who contribute to the research effort in learning and teaching. Systematic reflection on day-to-day practice with a view to trying to make improvements through analysing it can be presented as a different form of scholarship, which it certainly can be, as in action research. But there is a sense in which that kind of reflection must run through all the other forms of professional development if they are to be effective.

The essential point is that CPD is not and never can be homogeneous. It is simply a way of encouraging academics and support staff to include in their curiosity about their subject, curiosity about their own styles, methods and approaches to learning and transfer that to questions about students' learning.

With a little ingenuity it should be possible to promote something akin to Study Tours for CPD within the UK. It is not as if the American hosts to Study Tours thought they were doing anything exceptional. It was that what British academics and administrators saw and experienced was different from their own day-to-day experience. That was one thing. The other was that individuals in each group of four or five had time and space to mull things over in their own heads and with their fellow Study Tour members.

Although it has not been expressed explicitly, implicitly something of the kind has been going on for nearly forty years; peer reviews carefully organised and conducted in institutions and subjects. Every institutional or subject visit conducted under the aegis CNAA offered members of each panel an opportunity if they wanted to use it, to reflect on their own personal and institutional practice as they tried to understand and evaluate what institutions other than their own were doing. It was a form of unacknowledged staff development. Indeed the role of CNAA as a staff developer can be taken further. Every time a committee met, whether for policy or for consideration of some topic related to a subject, there were exchanges between professionals which had incalculable influences on what those professionals thought and did. If those reflections were set down on paper for subsequent analysis that is simply another way of looking at CPD.

Since the demise of CNAA the reviews conducted by the QAA and its attempts to create a set of benchmarks for each academic subject have implicitly contributed a form of staff development. But among the many differences between the operations of the CNAA and the QAA there is one element which redounds vitally on CPD. Whatever the complaints and resentment about the heavy handedness of CNAA there was a sense of the activities being owned by the academics who served on its various committees. Whether in committee considering new degree proposals or on panel visits to institutions academics were using the time and space thus spent to strive to come to some agreed professional judgements. This is an essential characteristic for successful CPD. To think without constraint about practice and as occasion presents to relate that to theory.

Unfortunately the QAA style of operation does not lend itself to a valuable form of staff development. Of course there is the same range of opportunities for reviewers to reflect on personal and institutional practice when talking with colleagues in another institution. But the unacceptable, often unproductive and much resented amount of paper work caused by the QAA operation limits those opportunities. Despite its claim to consult widely, academics acting as its assessors do not seem to have the same sense of collective ownership. Rather they perform according to template schemes drawn up by QAA staff, many of which are considered flawed by those self-same assessors. As a result the opportunities for both visiting reviewers and those being visited to learn from the occasion are restricted. The QAA could demonstrate its commitment to CPD by returning to a more collegiate style of activity. And this points to an important policy matter for the ILT. To be successful CPD has to be the personal property of individuals however it is recorded. Impositions are out.

Translated into the normal working of an institution, there are two lines for it to explore. There is the role of someone deputed to tend CPD within departments as missionaries for improvement in seeking to capitalise on those varied activities by academic staff. Heads of departments are probably too beset with bothers about numbers, resources, budgets and the Research Assessment Exercise to take on additionally what ought to be a consistently considerable load. Through them there can be arrangements for mentors in disciplines acting as well-placed advocates. And there is the obvious point that the more CPD is a linked in some way with a system of postgraduate qualifications and the reward system, the more attractive it will be for some members of that community. This is where AP(E)L can be put to serious work. Enabling academics to benefit directly from their own acquisition of further learning, however it is acquired, is based on sound educational principles. As many a practitioner can tell, as a mode of study AP(E)L can be far more effective than many a taught course.

Putting all that in the context of the CPD requirements for members to remain in good standing implies thinking further about possible ways of promoting a form of CPD which leads towards scholarship. Prescriptions are out. Set-piece courses clearly have a limited utility. When the educational equivalent to a new way of treating cancer comes along, then both for individual disciplines and learning and teaching development formal instruction makes sense. Instances of good practice put into circulation are unlikely to have much impact. Going on the success story of the Study Tours, limited visits by academics to something or some colleague which interests them in their own or a different institution with a little time to reflect on it can be guaranteed to produce learning and a sense of time being well spent. And that is what CPD is all about.

This could be pertinent to the huge problem of finding ways and means of exploiting the explosion of electronic communication techniques to support students' learning. Outright instruction in utilising the facilities offered by computers can save large amounts of time of the less-than-expert in understanding how to use the machine to the best advantage. But however careful and thorough may be the instruction, most novices find that being able to chat with a colleague about a problem, preferably when peering at the machine, is the fastest and best way of learning. This is no more and no less than peer group mentoring.

If this sounds woolly, vague and a way of evading difficult issues, it is not so. The simple point is that adults learn eclectically. Academics are bright by definition. But for CPD they are adults with the characteristics of adult learners. Pointing people in one direction is one thing. Telling them to follow that direction is something else and almost always fails. This after all is what academics imply when they use the rhetoric of self-directed learning for students, urging them to become independent learners. If they concentrate on what self-directed learning means for themselves then those with a teacher-led style and approach might review and adapt their practice. So CPD means that individual academics will take responsibility for what additional learning they find they need. How they learn it is no one else's business. What is someone else's business is some form of assurance that learning has occurred with notions of its applicability to improving students' learning.

Action research in education is a way of looking at this version of scholarship. It is reflection on practice, to recognise it, identify its strengths and weaknesses, and look for clues about possible ways of improvement in that practice. It can be either individual or group or team work. It is self-generating. To engage in action research means taking notes of practice as it goes along as the raw material for subsequent reflection. Thus is the engagement ensured of persons with activity. This constitutes a record of CPD in action which could easily become the basis for the verification which somehow has to meet the proper needs of the ILT.

This is all the more important since it is consistent with the ILT's stance of being a facilitator and not a regulator. As with submissions for accreditation institutions' views of CPD and how best it provides for its academic and support staff will vary. The common denominator has to be some form of reasonably accurate record keeping.

So the CPD requirements of the ILT for members to remain in good standing is one thing. What individuals choose to do is another. There can be no way requirements are translated into instructions to individuals as to what they are mandated to do. But there is a third dimension to CPD in relation to the ILT. And it is coming from the twenty-four centres, which make up the Learning and Teaching Support Network (LTSN), each in a different university, spread across England, Northern Ireland, Scotland and Wales. Some of the centres are to service a single subject like English or Engineering; some are to serve clusters of subjects like Medicine, Dentistry and Veterinary Medicine or Languages, Linguistics and Area Studies. Each centre is funded for five years from 2000.

All of the twenty-four centres have the same remit. Their so-called core activities are:

- setting up, supporting and developing learning and teaching networks;
- promoting and sharing good practices in learning, teaching and assessment;
- brokering the transfer of knowledge between users, experts, developers and innovators.

Those three activities are then expanded thus:
- collation of information on all aspects of teaching, learning and assessment;
- provision of staff development opportunities;
- advisory service to practitioners and departments;
- support through maintenance of networks and effective contacts;
- liaison with relevant professional bodies and subject associations;
- advice on the implementation of communication and information technologies in learning and teaching;
- ensuring that all practitioners and disciplines are aware of current and future developments in learning and teaching;
- collaboration with cognate subject centres to support inter-disciplinary and multidisciplinary activity;
- collaboration with the Generic Learning and Teaching Centre (GLTC) to ensure that subject centre staff are aware of broader issues.

Just to complete this picture of things to come, the GLTC has been set up in parallel with the LTSN. Its remit is: collating information in generic developments in teaching, learning and assessment; advising subject centres and HE institutions on generic teaching, learning and assessment issues, including the use of new technologies; maintaining an international outlook on generic learning and teaching developments; liaison with institutional learning and teaching bodies; staff development; liaison with the Joint Information Systems Committee (JISC) and other organisations managing research and development projects in learning and teaching; making available evaluations of generic communication and information technologies and teaching materials.

Between the two, the LTSN and the GLTC, a rich range of CPD additional possibilities is opened. It is possible, however, to see how institutions and their departments may be helped by those opportunities to promote CPD in directions which are beneficial for themselves as well as being, with a little persuasion perhaps, within the choice of individuals.

Suppose a department has identified important issues learned from a Quality Assurance Agency subject review. Suppose further that it proposes to tackle those issues instead of, as sometimes happens, taking the subject review as a necessary piece of window dressing after which things can revert to where they were before. Both the LTSN and the GLTC can offer an information system and all the other services listed under a centre's brief, but most importantly through networks they can facilitate connections with other academics in similar departments through telecommunication systems or direct in person. So it is possible to see an organic connection between QAA subject reviews, the developmental needs of an institution or department, those of individual academics and the CPD requirements of the ILT. This could be CPD with a bite.

But even this is not plain sailing. There is some suspicion. Some see the twenty-four centres of the LTSN and its companion the GLTC as a covert move towards centralisation. If publicly funded bodies are going to make pronouncements about the the best ways of teaching individual subjects to enhance students' learning, then even though announcements are being made by fellow academics, with the QAA in the background, is this a move towards establishing a national curriculum? Governments have denied any such intention in the past. The behaviour of the QAA does not remove the suspicion from the minds of some academics. Here is yet another tension that the ILT will have to live with.

To some extent the very fact that these developments are underway now is because some of the fierce competition between institutions which characterised much of the 1990s from the time polytechnics became universities is being replaced by a more collaborative stance. By extension it may not be too fanciful to see the internet becoming a reality Senior Common Room running across different institutions.

Although it is not mentioned in any of the consultative documents, AP(E)L as a theme runs through all these ways of looking at CPD. AP(E)L after all is nothing more than reflection on experience and identification of what has been learned from that experience. Unless records are merely going to be lists of activities undertaken there will have to be some evidence of thought. And since not only does the ILT brief make it clear that independent study is an essential component within CPD, but common sense suggests that for the majority of academic staff reflection is likely to be the most important element in their own CPD, some way will need to be evolved for recording it. This is no more than academics applying AP(E)L to themselves. In many ways the fast track can be seen as a forerunner of this kind of record keeping for CPD.

At this point it is worth registering that in some ways in some institutions AP(E)L is moving away from the periphery of things where it has rested since the early 1980s as something atypical from mainstream work, towards centre stage where it is seen as one form of assessment among many others. If that is true for undergraduate work, it must also be true for academic records of CPD. And that bears on record keeping.

The first thing to say about record keeping is that the ticks in boxes approach has no place in attempts to measure the effectiveness of CPD in contributing to an academic's professional development. Nothing could be more likely to disenchant the academic community and undermine its status in higher education as a whole. That is the negative of record keeping. The positive is that there are then two ways of looking at record keeping: individuals or institutions. The ILT is a membership professional organisation. CPD is a requirement for members to have their membership remain in good standing. That is an individual's responsibility. So record keeping of an individual's CPD is that individual's responsibility. The question then is who does the verifying. There are only two possibilities: the ILT itself or the individual's institution. The ILT could well find that an impossible administrative burden to carry. So could institutions. It is no good having reluctant policemen. The ILT will have to be very careful to avoid being over-prescriptive if it seeks help from institutions.

The positive way of looking at an institution's record keeping of CPD is that a university or college as an institution may wish to take an active role as part of its responsibility in promoting improvements in learning and teaching across its faculties and departments. In which case it would have a direct interest in keeping abreast of the efforts at improvement its academic staff is undertaking. It could see itself acting as the intermediary between individual member and ILT for verification. Whatever route is taken for record keeping, though, it needs to be record keeping with a very light touch.

There is of course another reason for institutions acting as verifier of their own academics' CPD. This goes back to Boyer's Scholarship of Teaching. Any university or college which is serious about enhancing the learning and teaching provided by its academics has to tackle the very difficult problem of creating a powerfully supportive atmosphere for encouraging improvements in learning and teaching. Almost certainly that means revising its policies for promotions and rewards. Combating Boyer's 'publish and get granted' culture and avoiding his stricture that it has devalued teaching and 'on many campuses it is a culture that restricts creativity rather than sustains it', implies just that. Excellence in helping students learn in classroom, laboratory or the field needs to take its place alongside publications, applications of knowledge and front-line research for new knowledge when it comes for consideration by promotions committees. Recommendations for promotion would need to be supported by records of CPD. Only then can academics begin to feel that research is not as Boyer put it 'the main route for the professoriate to gain status'. Their success as teachers and promoters of student learning would become a realistic alternative. And again as Boyer says, for many that would enable them to do what they came into teaching for: to offer a service as well as seeking a career.

Re-establishing that sense of offering a service as well as seeking a career is what the first set of awards under the National Teaching Fellowship Scheme could begin to do. Could, but not necessarily will. It all depends, as on so many other aspects of attempted improvements in higher education, on the status and standing which the ILT creates for itself. Funded jointly by the Higher Education Funding Council and the Department for Education and Employment, there were twenty scholarships awarded for the year 2000, each worth £50,000 which was to be ploughed back into their institutions for subsequent development. As if to make the point that it is enhancement of teaching in disciplines which is the key to improving students' learning the twenty awards ran right across the curriculum: history, science, languages, geography, linguistics, medical education, nursing, English, engineering, mathematics, music, student support services, information science, cultural studies, physiology, arts and psychology. What is more, the winners' institutions ran the gamut of all sorts; ancient, old, relatively new, quite new and colleges of higher education. And interestingly, three of the recipients were professors, three were at director of programme level, but the majority were lecturers in their subject. In every case the £50,000 Fellowship was going to pay for some innovative teaching scheme no matter what discipline. All were tuned to improving students' learning. Most concerned collaborative teams of academics. Each and every one would meet Boyer's Scholarship of Teaching. And perhaps most significant of all, the awards were not seen by the recipients as personal accolades, but as tributes to the profession of teaching. They said so. Not before time, many would say. But it can be taken as a tiny step towards the Dearing intention of raising the status of teaching. As such it is a modest indication of national support from the highest levels for CPD for teachers in higher education from its paymasters. Institutions take note.

To follow the Boyer line is not unlike the proposed development of pay policies for school teachers. Excellence in the classroom is being signalled as a route to promotion and pay increases parallel to the traditional one of career development through climbing the hierarchy of becoming a head of department, then a deputy headship and then a headship. Applying the same principle to academics could mean that there should be a larger number of Readerships. It could mean the reinstatement of positions such as Professor of Science Education. But any move to widen the route to promotion within an institution is bound to add spice and motivation for many to the overall concept of CPD.

There is a final comment to make. One of the more curious implications of public policies which focus on the need to ensure proper standards and so ensure improvements is a tendency to speak as though improvements were on an exponential upwards path with perfection at its zenith. Perfection is not attainable in learning and teaching any more than it is in primary school scores in literacy or numeracy, or in A level grades, or in medical treatment or policing, or anywhere else for that matter. For higher education improvement comes from two directions. There is keeping up-to-date with developments in an individual's own discipline, sustaining an expertise, which comes from all the usual forms of formal study – books, journals, lectures, professional association activities. Then there is working out how best to use that up-to-date knowledge in the service of helping the increasingly heterogeneous student body to learn. And for both there are no absolute standards. Whereas it may be possible to assess pretty accurately the subject up-to-date-ness of an individual academic there is no reliable ready reckoner which can assess definitively the effectiveness of that individual' s teaching.

The mysterious mixture of art, skill and knowledge which constitutes teaching and hence learning can only be viewed subjectively. Student evaluations and peer observations can produce subjective judgements. But the variables affecting the teaching and learning being observed can be quite dramatically different from one year to another – different composition of the student group, different room accommodation, different time of the day or week – so that at worst last year's improvement can look like this year's deterioration, or at best this year's improvement is particularly noticeable. But everlasting improvement is not available.

Improvements through CPD depend on the scope and quality of thought which goes into an academic's contribution to learning through teaching. That is the central purpose of CPD. That is what the ILT exists to promote. Boyer's Scholarship of Teaching needs to be its watchword.

10 Where next for the ILT?

Implementing the vision

- Enhancing the status of teaching.
- Improving the experience of teachers.
- Supporting innovation in higher education.

That is where next. Except that it seems a bit odd that enhancing student learning is not part of that declared vision. Of course it is implied, but it is the object of the entire enterprise. The question is how is the ILT going to promote the improved learning and teaching for students as it seeks to turn the vision into reality. Implicitly it involves institutional change. The claim of this book is that AP(E)L can help to get it there. There is a second claim. That is that CPD can be seen as a way of broadening the concept of what all teaching encompasses and of tackling the essential issue for the ILT: how best continuing professional development can be done.

The ILT will be able to quote numbers of members with waiting lists for acceptance. It will be able to cite the number of institutions which have submitted staff development programmes for accreditation. Some twenty-two of the top fifty recruiting universities are said to be participants. Members have come from twenty-two of the pre-1992 universities, twenty-one of the post-1922 universities and seven colleges or institutes of higher education. It can list the activities which it has promoted – conferences, articles, meetings and the like. But of themselves that can mean something or nothing. There are a whole host of reasons why either can be the case.

The enhancement of the status of teaching depends to a large extent not on the numbers of academic and support staff who become members of the ILT nor the numbers of institutions in contact with it. The critical factor will be how it is perceived by the academic community as a whole. In its turn for some that will depend on how academics rate the services which the ILT offers them in terms of engaging them in activities which they believe connect with their day-to-day activities, giving them a sense of doing their job better. For others not interested in its services, their continuing membership is likely to depend on the publicly recognised status the ILT achieves.

To this end, the ILT's Website announces two significant developments. As from early in 2001 a new membership category will be launched – Associateship. Criteria and procedures will be similar to those for full membership but with the following variation. Applicants will be asked to produce evidence 'only' of the first four requirements for membership: teaching and learning support; design and planning of activities; assessment and feedback given to learners; developing effective learning environments and learner systems, along with 'the processes of reflective practice and personal development'. There is to be an Individual Entry Route and an Institutional Accreditation Route. Anyone going for the Individual Entry Route will need to have had the equivalent of one year's experience of learning support. And as befits the lower level than membership, the fee for the Individual Entry Route is predicted at £25 and an annual subscription of £40. All staff whatever their seniority are encouraged to apply, with a rather odd addition that pathways will be developed to allow '. . . to move between membership categories, in either direction, as their careers evolve'. This amounts to a serious move to widen the membership of the ILT while bolstering its status.

The other move is of a different order: the ILT's Council Elections. The announcement says '. . . steps are now being taken to encourage members to become active in the organisation for election to the ILT Council, the ruling body of the ILT. This accords with the Memorandum and Articles of Association which provide the legal basis for the operation of the ILT.' According to the rubric, by December 2000 the Council would be in being with its first body of elected members. At which point the profession itself will begin to muse about its status.

When it turns its attention to the second of the items of the vision – improving the experience of teaching – it will confront one of those delightfully ambiguous headlines which can be interpreted in as many ways as there are interpreters. It certainly does not mean an easier life. If anything it means the opposite. Any university or college Senior Common Room hears stories which are a coded way of saying that it is highly gratifying when students show that they have learned what it was hoped they would learn, and that they showed every sign of enjoying how they learned it. That is an element in improving the experience of teaching. Where that occurs in all probability it was the result of carefully considered preparation, not just of the content to be handled but the ways in which it would be made accessible to students most effectively. All that plus a feeling in that group of students that they are participants and not just recipients. In an ideal world all academics would feel that way about some of their teaching, with staff and students basking in a holy glow of effective learning. So, for any general improvement in the experience of teaching more academics will have to find more interesting ways of engaging students. How to do that is the conundrum which the ILT is intended to tackle. It begins to touch some of the requirements for membership. And it is central to the role of CPD.

If supporting innovation in learning and teaching in higher education is to be more than a vacuous pious hope, then it means grappling with questions of institutional change. And that implies going way beyond encouraging academics and support staff to become members of the ILT or submitting programmes for accreditation. Not to go beyond that runs expensive and potentially damaging risks. It is disastrous to have enthusiasts for improving their teaching who feel that they are left on the sidelines. Without strong leadership that is a substantial risk. And with pressures on resources for new initiatives like the e-university it is easy for attention on teaching and learning to be shunted into a siding. The educational world is littered with examples of such side lining which results in developers, actual and potential, seeing their superiors as cynical obstructionists to anything they do not want for any number of sometimes idiosyncratic reasons. The stakes are too high in higher education for that risk to be taken, save by default. That is merely sub-set to a larger range of risks. For many an institution not going beyond encouraging membership of the ILT risks its very existence. For those, institutional change needs to be at the top of the agenda.

This in no way ignores the very substantial institutional change which has run through higher education in the last fifteen or so years. Some changes have applied to all universities and colleges, such as the levying of fees on students. All have had some level of reorganisation thrust on them as a result of reduced funding. But some have shifted from a linear wallpaper pattern of academic curricula to a modular curriculum to support a credit accumulation system. Some, not all, it is important to note. Some had no need to. It did not fit. Where that shift did take place it was because the institution felt it needed to do so to extend the range of learning opportunities available to students so that they could compose their own learning programmes which best suited them. It was also to take account of the domestic and financial circumstances of the increasing number of older students within the study body so as to provide stopping off and stepping in points within a formal programme leading to a higher education qualification. Those stopping off and stepping in points were also introduced with an eye on possible changes to the attendance patterns of students as they tended to work more to help reduce their dependence on student loans. Alternating periods of study and employment are likely to become the norm for huge rafts of students, if not the majority. And, of course, in consonance with one of the themes in this book, some adopted both AP(E)L and WBL. The question is what kind of match will be there be between Dearing's hope for ILT membership becoming the 'norm' for academics and the 'norm' prevalent in the student body?

For improvements, AP(E)L gives some clues. AP(E)L schemes up and down the country give evidence that entries based on lower than the usually required academic qualifications can result in degree classifications which are generally in line, and sometimes better than those of traditional entrants. Where that is the case almost always it is the result of providing appropriate student support services as well as using learning and teaching styles which are tuned to the needs, conditions and stage of development of those students. Recognising previous learning accomplishments as the basis for further acquisition of knowledge and skill, recognising that a range of learning styles exists in any one group of students is basic to success in any form of learning provision. AP(E)L and WBL programmes offer proof of that, were proof needed, and so can offer models of how to do it.

The reason for those developments was that far more attention was paid to the needs of students as learners than tends to be the case for the more conventional students. For a start, inviting students to produce evidence for themselves of what they had learned already, without knowing it, and having it recognised and valued by academics in an academic institution sent a very different message from the standard admissions wording. Having recruited people like that it was obvious that they would need considerable help to articulate that experiential learning either in group work or individual tutorials. So AP(E)L reinforced the case which was growing anyway, for a better set of student services to cope with the widening differentiation within student cohorts. And all of that contributes to improving both learning and teaching.

However, apart from AP(E)L and WBL, all the other elements in institutional change do not of themselves introduce improvements in learning and teaching. They create a framework for and offer encouragement for seeking improvements. Indeed for some they are essential preconditions for doing so. What then looks like being the next stage in institutional change? What sort of innovation can be expected to meet the rather grandiose banner of the ILT? And what of AP(E)L in innovation? And wherein lies the improvement of learning and teaching?

First the context. According to the Basic Skills Agency (BSA) some 24% of adults in England are in one way or another functionally illiterate and that the same proportion of the adult population is functionally innumerate. As if to ram the point home, the OECD comparative study of twenty countries puts Britain at the bottom of the list when compared with other Anglo-Saxon areas and European countries. Even worse is that whereas these deficiencies in other countries are bunched on older people, in Britain those literacy and numeracy problems run across the entire age range. Whatever the doubts about the methodology of compiling those figures, the UK story remains rather depressing

That is the background against which to see government policies for the expansion of numbers in higher education to 50% of an age cohort, if the Prime Minister's pronouncement is taken at its face value. It is also the reality that policies for the promotion of Lifelong Learning seek to confront.

That is fact. There is another fact which both the general public and much of higher education has yet to grasp. That is that attainment at exit is more important than performance at entry. Results matter more than how they are acquired. Concentration on entry qualifications supports and encourages the perception that higher education is for an elite. This is a very hard perception to change, but it is something which a mass system requires should change. It is not as if there is no evidence to support that shift. It is a question of willingness to see it. This applies particularly to some of the professions.

This now moves on to the student body. Tuition fees have to be the starting point. There was bound to be a slow beginning to the long-term academic consequences of that policy change once the arguments are over as to whether there ought to be any dues levied on students at all. Applicants will get more choosy. They will want to feel that their money is being well spent. Already many students choose to apply to institutions because they like the look of the courses on offer rather than the institution's reputation or geographical location. The potential scholars will go as they always have to high level research universities. And so they should. But for most in the mass system it is the likelihood of attaining a high level of employability which is influential in calculating their approach to the admission stakes.

But attractively presented courses in brochures, handbooks and prospectuses can only be successful courses if the students feel that they are being well taught and learn what they anticipated learning, or if not that then something which satisfies them. Increasingly they are equipped with a set of learning outcomes for each course so that what they are expected to know and be able to do at the end of a course is set out for them to read in advance. And this is where ideas about improving the quality of learning and teaching begin to bite. All the usual things come into the reckoning here, like sticking to the syllabus rather than following some hare of particular interest to the tutor, clear presentation of material, marking schedules adhered to, and the heinous crime of reading last year's notes; or worse, quoting extensively and even reading sections of a book written by the tutor. These are used by students to reckon up the quality of a course they are following. Increasingly if they do not like what they are offered, the news will spread around, recruitment can drop, course closure gets discussed and maybe redundancy beckons.

For students, it is worth asking the question, where are they as well as who are they? Long gone are the days of a residential three years being the normal way of studying at a university or college. Going too are the days when it is sufficient for institutions to assume that the students they want will come and attend classes on campus. The experience of some institutions of offering courses and classes off campus in business or manufacturing premises, suggests that in some areas this kind of provision needs energetic development. As the average age of the student population rises so this approach to providing higher education is set to become more significant.

If not at work students may be at home. Telecommunications and the internet stand as a kind of sub-set of the off-campus provision of learning. Apart from some major providers, full-scale distance learning facilities offered through the internet are beyond the reach of most institutions. They can enable their students to make use of what is on offer through telecommunication, but it will be as well to keep reality learning in perspective. Facilities must be there. Increasingly students expect them to be there. They are telling supplements to what institutions and their tutors can offer. Only in rare cases and for rare people can it be a substitute. But of course in terms of informal learning the internet has huge significance. This adds a whole raft of possibilities for informal learning but no one has the faintest idea of the range and scope of it. Or they may be in full-time or part-time work. For them a mixture of courses offered on the employers' premises, on-campus courses and a variety of ways of incorporating WBL in certificates, diplomas and degrees. Exactly where these potential students will be in the future it is impossible to know. All there is to be sure about is that attendance patterns will change. There will be more stepping in, stepping on and stepping out of programmes than at present. Accommodating that is an institutional matter, and for many requires significant change. For increasing numbers of students, the programme needs to be self-paced. Some will find it on the telecommunications systems which institutions are fast developing. And without a modular structure for academic study with a credit accumulation system it is not easy to see how that can be provided. Probably the QAA needs to pay more attention than it does currently to all that in the interests of learning and teaching.

Then there are the implications of continuing expansion. Without going into all the in's and out's of the year-by-year improvement in A level scores, it is obvious that if more higher education places are available then more will be taken up by men and women who have low rather than high A level scores. That in no way implies that they are bound to produce lower results than their higher scoring peers, any-more than it implies that many older students without the standard entry requirements do worse in their studies than younger apparently better qualified students. What it does draw attention to however is that the continuing expansion means expanding comparably the range of effective student support services. Complaints that schools are failing to prepare their pupils properly for degree level study may or may not be true. But they are irrelevant. Expansion continues and there are few signs that it will go into reverse. If it does not, whether they like it or not institutions will have to develop their support services, whether counselling, academic advising, learning support, financial guidance and the one-to-one contact which can make all the difference to student performance. It needs to put imagination to work. Like the one stop shop advocated for benefits and employment offices, joined up support services for students are likely to be more effective than several different specialist offices. It is so easy to over-estimate the ability of students to use facilities which exist to help them and to underestimate their diffidence and reluctance to use them. And that provision is not just a professional requirement in the service of students. It is also a piece of self-serving. Somehow institutions have to keep the drop out and withdrawal rates as low as possible despite the changing nature of the student body, to sustain their level of funding from the Funding Councils. It is another way of talking about institutional change.

So the third issue is a question rather than fact: how best to serve that wide range of students? If institutional change can provide no more than conditions for conducive improvements in learning and teaching, the focus falls on individual tutors and support staff and how they do their job of serving students. At which stage the AP(E)L strand which runs through the consultative documents for the creation of the ILT becomes extremely interesting and perhaps suggestive.

The open question is the extent to which the procedures for seeking membership of the ILT will influence the approach that academics adopt to the learning of their students. More narrowly for the theme of this book, how far will the experience of AP(E)L, either through the fast track arrangements or through the AP(E)L route for an accredited course, affect their perception of student learning. Having experienced for themselves the intellectual demands made by undertaking AP(E)L, having, one hopes, enjoyed the satisfactions it can bring and then feeling gratified at results, do they view their task of promoting student learning differently?

That may be narrowing the focus on the results of one element in the membership rules for the ILT but it is a very widely focused question. A 50% participation rate means a wider range of entry qualifications, a wider range of the experiences of learning, and a wider range of capacities and abilities among the young men and women who arrive at a university or college. It is important to remember that none of that means necessarily a reduction of standards. But as A level scores and tallies may continue to rise, while for many of the successful ones this will have been as a result of excellent teaching, it is likely to have been of an essentially didactic style. In the best sixth forms and in different departments within schools, that is not the case, but generally a large proportion of first-year students in higher education have had little or no experience of participatory learning. Indeed, sometimes in higher education there is a complaint that they do not seem interested in learning at all. They just want instruction. This raises questions about student motivation. If having had years of the *tabular rasa* style of tuition they find that that is what greets them in their first-year courses, the chances are that their motivation as learners drops. They can feel disappointed. The excitement of being in higher education can get dampened. Some step out, although no one knows how many of them step in later. But drop-out figures can then affect an institution's funding.

Put differently, this points to a curricula issue. As many an academic has observed it is and has been the case for a long time that for significant proportions of the student body, the standard ways of learning in higher education through lectures and laboratories as the sole means of learning are inappropriate and to some extent ineffective even. By the end of two years, many a student has had enough and will say so. But time and again the experience coming from projects in higher education shows that it is a mixture of learning in classrooms with some form of learning in the real world of any kind of work which suits their learning needs best. And it sustains their formal academic learning. This is Work-Based Learning with AP(E)L as its partner. It is WBL organised and facilitated through AP(E)L. Add in the rich possibilities through the internet and websites and the opportunities multiply impressively of meeting students' needs for learning.

If that has been the case for some time, it becomes a much more serious matter with the prospect of widening participation rates further up to 50%. It is a serious curriculum issue. Now curriculum issues only get tackled when academics feel the need to do so. Curriculum revision is well nigh continuous in some disciplines as research findings wend their way into professional journals and conferences and so into the discussions of course committees in institutions. But starting at the other end, thinking not of courses provided but of the recipients – the students – can produce a different conception of curriculum development. Asking the question how do these students learn best is a pedagogical question not a content question. If the answer is the mixture of formal tuition and off-campus learning, articulating that answer is a vital curriculum issue. Curriculum change is the way of producing that articulation. The central answer to those questions is the extent to which academics are prepared to ask those curriculum questions and revise accordingly. Further, how far they are willing to undertake the additional forms of learning on which WBL is based. For the ILT the question will be to what extent has the experience of membership contributed to these kinds of curricula and institutional change.

It is not an easy business, anymore than establishing reliable telecommunication systems is easy. It is cheaper however. WBL and AP(E)L changes the role of many tutors. It has been said so many times that it is almost boring to say it again. Instead of being distributors of knowledge in familiar circumstances they become facilitators of learning in both familiar and unfamiliar settings. It is the unfamiliar setting which is the nub of the matter for this form of curriculum revision. It means reorganising work timetables and tutorial load to cope with the demands made by WBL. It means accepting the proposition that nowadays learning occurs all over the place and that it is its assessment which matters not where it comes from. There is further the acceptance of another proposition; that intentional learning at work can be organised and can be significant at higher education levels. There are employers to deal with. There are learning agreements with students and employers to negotiate. There is the supervision of the learning in work placements to monitor. More important than anything there is the design of a set of learning outcomes which can be applied to any and every work setting, and the criteria and procedures to be used in assessing that learning. That last is the really critical element because it links WBL with the institution's quality assurance mechanisms and provides the rationale for arguing the case for WBL whether within or without the university or college.

It is easy when talking about the 50% participation rate proposal to forget that that is not talking only about increasing the numbers of school leavers who go on to higher education. A fair expectation is that there will be more older students following the tendency recorded in many institutions that numbers of older students increase year by year and in some cases are in the majority. Part-time study is then bound to increase. Much of that will be to accommodate the domestic, economic, social and employment circumstances of people in full-time work. And part-time work. No one can predict, though many make prophetic comments, about the way the world of work is going to develop over the next generations. All we can know is that work life will not be the same as it is today. Against that much of higher education has to make its dispositions to equip it for whatever kind of student body comes along. Part of that re-equipping concerns curriculum revision and bringing WBL and with it AP(E)L into the regular provision. These are ways of contributing to the essentials; fitting what an institution has to offer to the circumstances of its students. In no way does this imply reducing academic standards or dumming down. It is a pedagogical shift to facilitate the learning of large numbers of students.

There is then the fascinating issue of informal learning. Where will the ILT stand in relation to that? Nobody disputes that a great deal of informal learning goes on. It may be through voluntary or community organisations. It may be through clubs – sports, fishing, play reading, book readings, gardening. It may be through private learning to follow a personal inclination, say cooking, wine tasting, DIY. But in this country we do not know for sure how prevalent are those forms of informal learning. What we do know is that on the whole the formal education system tends to view informal learning as a kind of anteroom to its own formal provision rather than something which exists in its own right.

That view is articulated where an institution offers AP(E)L facilities. In a surprising number of cases what has been acquired informally turns out to have some academic significance, something which under-lines the importance for numbers of institutions of developing AP(E)L programmes. That however does nothing to sort out the relationship between informal and formal learning, if indeed there needs to be one beyond saying that both exist but separately. The difficulty with that in general is that formal education tends to undervalue informal education which does neither any good.

This becomes important when institutions take policies for Lifelong Learning into account. The full title of the Dearing Report was Higher Education in a Learning Society. Throughout, the report doffed its cap towards Lifelong Learning. Although the report made no specific connections between its recommendation for the ILT and Lifelong Learning, the significance of that proposal takes on an urgency when seen in the context of a mass higher education system. Widening access and increasing participation means that the student population will cover ever widening sections of the community. That is the deliberate intention of current policies. But it is equally important to remember that different and less favoured backgrounds and school experience do not necessary mean lower attainment levels, an argument which gets tangled with issues of academic standards and quality. The experience of the Open University over the last thirty years ought to settle that argument.

So far government pressure for more Lifelong Learning concentrates on formal classes which lead to an official qualification and can be funded through measurable results. But that is only half the issue. Life-long Learning as a national programme means having more people learning more throughout their lives. One consequence of that is that the skills and knowledge in the workforce get a boost which is neces-sary for economic survival. However, that is not much good unless the Lifelong Learning also contributes to people's social and personal sense of well-being. And since it is clear that a great deal of personal satisfaction comes from informal learning, separate from formal learning it may be, but significant it assuredly is.

For higher education, that poses the question: Does it have any role in helping to promote and encourage informal learning? The connection through AP(E)L is obvious. But beyond that, what if anything ought universities and colleges to be doing? They might create internal units with a brief to get out and about to encourage informal learning of all kinds on the assumption that that could be a route to additional sources of recruitment. That raises awkward questions of funding. But it is not easy to think of anything which implies action. Obviously the more encouragement there is for individuals to make connections between their informal learning and formal learning in formal education institutions the better. That goes back to the public perception of a particular institution, how welcoming it is seen to be. But it also suggests that where a university or college teams up with another body – formal, voluntary, community – and shows itself in places where people live and work, the more encouragement there will be. So much of that depends on an institution's history, its geographical position, its internal organisation. Even more it depends on some academics believing that that is something important for them to do.

Resources is the last issue for trying to improve the services for learning and teaching for the more heterogeneous student body. That has to be an institutional matter. Allocations of tutorial time for WBL need to be realistic if the curriculum is to fulfil its promise. There are added minor costs associated with any off-campus scheme. It may be that in all, providing a WBL course is more expensive than a regular classroom course. That becomes the key institutional decision. This is the sort of hard decision which lies at the heart of any successful curriculum development. It is the same with telecommunication systems. Can they not be afforded? If more resources are going to WBL or telecommunication then less resources go elsewhere. Measured against enrolments, however, it may appear to be a wise way of using resources, however limited.

This is further complicated because those kinds of developments imply a different distribution overall of academics' time – what they spend their time actually doing. If the range of learning styles students display theoretically can be matched with different facilities for learning which their developments introduce, turning that theoretical position into the day-to-day experience of students inevitably means that time allocated to formal tuition, academic support, internet time, is bound to be rejigged. One way and another it means teaching less and supporting more. It ought to mean too more support staff are available to academic staff to free them from what are essentially office jobs like duplicating and so on so that they can get on and do what they are employed to do – teaching students. And that too implies a shift in the distribution of resources. That is not a welcome prospect for many, but in one or another it is the price of seeking improvements to learning and teaching. And CPD relates to all of the possible developments of institutions, of the curriculum and of the stance and attitude of individual academics.

The need for institutions to go down these routes is prodded from three separate directions. All raise fears of overcentralisation and so the sapping of institutional autonomy. The ILT needs to take this very seriously. Creeping centralisation of education has long had a bad name and it has been progressive. Without going into the long story from the scrapping of the Schools Council for Curriculum Reform and Examinations, from the Education Reform Act of 1988 onwards and particularly for higher education since the scrapping of CNAA in 1992, government edicts have been fired at schools, further and higher education institutions. And progressively for the teachers at all levels and to differing extents it has felt as if they were being reduced to technicians for carrying out preordained tasks by governments in a panicky anxiety to achieve improvements. And now the sector can only wait and see what is envisaged for them with the Learning and Skills Council with a remit to involve universities in its regional efforts to enhance the skills of the workforce.

There is the question of funding from the Funding Councils which, under pressure from government, could well take its criteria into these areas. And there are the different though related pressures coming from the Quality Assurance Agency and the Qualifications and Curriculum Authority. Provided that all revisions to what an institution offers and how it offers it are conducted under the scrutiny of an institution's quality assurance procedures the QAA's requirements can be met. But lurking in the shadows there are signs that the QCA may wish to be involved with some of the qualifications which emerge from CPD. This would seem irrelevant to institutional provision of existing higher education qualifications, certificates, diplomas and degrees. But unless there is strong collaboration between higher education and the professions it is easy to see that vocational qualifications could emerge which would be the concern of the QCA. No doubt for some this would be a welcome development. For others it could be yet another unwelcome intrusion.

All this connects with the ILT and the third fear. There are fears about the introduction of some form of compulsory accreditation for teachers in higher education. When the Dearing Report referred to the hope that in the future membership of the ILT would be the 'norm' for academics in higher education perhaps that was a deliberate piece of trail blazing. To some extent the success or the failure of the ILT as a membership organisation to realise its vision will depend on its ability to protect the integrity of its individual members as professionals.

- Enhancing the status of teaching
- Improving the experience of teachers
- Supporting innovation in higher education

That is the vision. Membership of the ILT assumes a commitment from its members to that vision. Obviously all three elements of the vision overlap. As a peer group organisation its contribution to enhancing the status of teaching depends to a large extent on its standing with the academic community as a whole. And that depends on its usefulness for academics. Clearly the status of teaching will be enhanced at a personal level if it becomes more satisfying and enjoyable and that in turn depends on innovations their institutions may introduce. At a public level it will be enhanced to the extent that government can be convinced that academics are meeting the needs of the ever-changing society. The same applies to employers and the general public. It could be too that higher education's inclusion in the General Teaching Council offers in the long term another vehicle for enhancing its status.

Improving the experience of teaching is a far more subjective matter. It is no good trying to base improvements on better terms of employment. In the present circumstances improvements in that experience can only come through the personal satisfaction which results from students becoming more effective, more enthusiastic learners, which in turn is derived from innovations in ways of promoting students' learning. That is a tough proposition if ever there was one. But going on the experience of many academic staff in higher education working on schemes of AP(E)L and WBL it enhances their pleasure because its very activity is different from classroom and laboratory routines, acting like a blood transfusion for their professional work. One test for the ILT is the extent that it can support, encourage, even introduce innovative schemes which pave the way for that satisfaction. But in turn again that depends to a large extent on innovations undertaken at an institutional level.

What may be the longer term influence of the LTSN and the GLTC can only be speculation. But it is reasonable to suppose that they will both fail unless they can contribute to the enjoyment of teaching, enriching it as an experience, through the various facilities they offer. If they do turn out to be valued by academics it is reasonable to suppose that the appetite can be whetted for trying things out in the search for improvement.

As for innovations themselves, they depend on an institution's circumstances, how it perceives its purpose, and the willingness of its academic and support staff to support innovations which are often personally uncomfortable. They can raise important questions which offend against proven ways of teaching and learning. They can therefore raise questions of principle about the application of some innovations for particular disciplines. But they also depend on senior staff, professors and heads of department taking seriously innovatory ideas thought up by colleagues however junior they may be, and making colleagues believe they are open to them, even if they do not actually welcome them.

The claim of this book is that AP(E)L is involved with every part of that vision. It goes back to the first consultations about the establishment of the ILT itself. It runs through the procedures for acquiring membership of the ILT. The most significant innovations both for the curriculum and institutions are likely to involve AP(E)L and WBL in one way or another. To a very large extent innovations of that kind will come from individuals. So another test for the ILT will be the extent to which the experience of membership and CPD requirements enthuses individual academics to promote the cause for innovation within their own institution.

As with so many innovatory bodies, money is going to be one of the most difficult issues to deal with. Entrance fees stand at £25. Annual membership stands at £75 and is tax deductible as for the membership fees of any professional organisation. In many institutions first time joiners under the fast track arrangements are having their fees paid in full or in part along with the entrance fee. With membership fees standing at £85 there is no means of knowing the proportion of early members who will decide to keep up their membership annually.

That is at an individual level. Once institutions have paid their fees for the accreditation of their own professional courses which lead to membership, no further income comes from them

For the ILT itself on the other side, the fast track accreditation system is expensive. The £25 fee for entry to membership cannot possibly cover the costs of fast track procedures, with its three-decker arrangement for scrutiny. The calculation must have been that in the first instance to get the largest possible number of members in the shortest possible time, the fast track was a loss leader, worth offering in the expectation of better things to come. But as a publicly funded body, the more income it can raise itself the greater its self-confidence and its ability to resist any attempts at external inference.

There are two words which relate to the idea of enhancing the status of teaching in higher education and for that matter of all teachers. They are 'professional' and 'vocational'. According to the Oxford Dictionary, profession means 'vocation or calling especially of a learned or scientific artistic kind (divinity, the law and medicine)' and 'members of such a calling collectively'. Teaching does not feature among those callings. Professional is then 'of the vocations called professional'. The list of activities which are called professions has exploded exponentially as different groups have sought to lift their own status. So without altering its meaning the nature of that meaning has been diluted. Teaching has suffered from that dilution even when remembering that teaching has never been rated very highly as an occupation in this country. There is a semantic puzzle here too which may be a substantive issue as well. Higher education academics are appointed as lecturers. There is little doubt that for some that induces a lecture led mode and style whereas the details of day-to-day teaching and learning get less emphasis. Similarly, the use of the word vocation has spread so widely that apart from the priesthood and the religious it is difficult to use it now to describe any work activity as a calling. Vocational is now linked to employability. Vocation or a calling now sounds positively antediluvian when discussing any professional activity.

But enhancing the status of teaching implies re-establishing the sense that while 'research and publication have become the primary means by which most professors achieve academic status', they are not the only way of achieving professional advancement, and sustaining the motives of academics who 'are drawn to the profession precisely because of their love for teaching and service'.

Interpreted in a severely strict way that is another way of talking about calling. As Boyer put it, that is the way to correct what in many campuses 'has devalued teaching and on many campuses it is a culture that restricts creativity rather than sustains it.'

If the Dearing Committee or its theoretical successor were to report during 2001, would it make a recommendation for the Institute of Learning and Teaching? In the light of the convincing evidence that postgraduate and post-experience courses for professional development are now common in institutions rather than exceptions, in some ways the answer could be no. A different question is whether without the establishment of the ILT the proliferation of those courses would have occurred. And the answer to that must be doubtful. There is no doubt that staff for professional and education development in institutions feel that they have been given a powerful external boost. And to that extent it has to be the case that their efforts have been given an additional licence and encouragement internally. Institutions themselves are keeping a weather eye on the Higher Education Funding Council to see how far membership numbers will affect funding allocations. So the initial thrust and enthusiasm given by many to the ILT means that it may be on the way to getting itself established soundly.

Perhaps the best answers to the question: Where next? come from academics who have had the experience of either taking a full course leading to membership of SEDA and therefore having automatic eligibility for ILT membership, or applicants who have used the fast track procedures. One of the strongest impressions gained from academics who have gone down the fast track route to membership of the ILT is that what they value most is the requirement to reflect. Reflection in the context of learning and teaching in higher education means thinking about day-to-day practice, whether it be activities in the classroom or laboratory, preparation, assessing students' work, supporting students in their work, revising courses and keeping them up to date, collaborating in team work, managing departments or functioning at an institutional level. And again and again the comment is that thinking about any of those aspects of their work is precisely what gets squeezed out in the sheer pressure of events. Larger student groups with heavier marking loads, numerous committee meetings, quality assurance visits; the list is endless of the demands made of their time which leaves totally inadequate time to think about what they are doing. But also time and again academics say that they acknowledge it is vital to find time for reflection, and from more senior people that opportunities for groups of academics to get together to discuss matters of mutual interest is something which they have to attend to. But this very reaction indicates part of the toll being taken for creating a mass system with annually declining staff–student ratios. If through its CPD arrangements the ILT can do anything to help people create time and space for that kind of reflection it will be doing something useful for the academic community.

In earlier times when academic life ran at a less frenetic pace, the Senior Common Room was a regular meeting place for academics. A cup of coffee, armchairs to sprawl in, newspapers and journals to read; and there was always a sprinkling of men and women who talked about their day-to-day practice in conversational terms, and the exchanges often ran across disciplines, just as they often turned into unofficial departmental meetings. This was not something which was organised; it just happened, no doubt with some pressure on some to be there. But essentially it just happened. It was not labelled staff development, let alone CPD but in effect that is what is was. It was systematic reflection on experience which is AP(E)L before the notion was conceptualised.

That is no longer possible. Even if a Senior Common Room can be found, such is the pressure on accommodation, it would be unlikely to find many people in it, let alone groups of people from the same department. Credit accumulation and modular courses have demolished the kind of timetable which created the time and space for such meetings. Most complain that time is so filled that it is all they can do to get there in the morning and leave exhausted at the end of the day for the homeward journey. As remarked earlier, perhaps the internet is a partial replacement for the twenty-first century.

These are the circumstances in which the ILT was born and now has its being. This is the world it has stepped into. So maybe a very important part of the answer to the Where next? question is to see the ILT 's promotion and encouragement of systematic reflection as one way of trying to the fill the vacumn left by the demise of those earlier times when conversations about pedagogy and methodology were something taken for granted without any po-faced labelling. And just as the sharpest hindsight has to recognise that there were significant numbers of academics who reflected little if at all on what they were appointed to do, so in the future there are bound to be academics who do not take the trouble to reflect. That does not mean abandoning the noble intention of it becoming the 'norm' for academics to be members of the ILT. It does mean that the more who do so are likely to think more systematically about how to fulfil their professional responsibilities.

But the larger part of the answer to the Where next? question is the extent to which reflecting on their own practice and thinking about how to improve it, deepens and expands academics' understanding of how they themselves learn and how far that can be translated into perceptions of students' approaches to learning. This, after all, is the assessment of prior experiential learning at work. It is full circle. Twenty years after AP(E)L first became a topic of discussion on the edges of higher education. To the extent that academics can develop reflection in their students, the quality of learning will be enhanced. And incidentally it relates to some of the curriculum demands about employability.

Recruitment of academic staff may, just may, seem a long way away from the ILT trying to realise its vision. But there are growing anxieties about the recruitment of academics. The age profile of existing staff means that soon there will be a large gap left as experienced older academics retire. Here is another part of the unscripted brief for the ILT. Above all if it can succeed in not only improving the status of teaching, but somehow helping to enrich teaching as an enjoyable way of earning a living, it may help recruitment. To that end perhaps it may also do something to encourage the view that teaching can be accurately described as a vocation as well as a profession.

Put together the stimulus offered by the Teaching Fellowship Scheme, with the developments which the LTSN and GLTC can offer, it could all mesh with the ILT's CPD requirements. Soon visual connections through the ether will supplement the current voice and text exchanges. Perhaps through all those facilities it is not too far-fetched to think of networking through the internet as a reinstatement in a twenty-first century form of a Senior Common Room. Part of realising the vision might be to see academics sprawled in armchairs long distances apart chatting about this and that instead of moving the chairs in a Common Room. Virtual reality of CPD.

Anything of the sort would go some way to meeting the responses of academics who have been through a SEDA accredited course. Novices and those with relatively short experience who had followed courses emphasised that it was the group discussions which were most valuable. 'At the time I found some of the discussion stimulating. Hearing about problems, concerns, issues and solutions from people in other departments was reassuring to me.' And, 'I particularly enjoyed and benefited from the peer observation we carried out . . . it would have been nice to have more of this exercise.' Another said, 'Understanding the differences and similarities between the perspectives across the disciplines' was the best part.'

It is difficult for senior academics to feel any sense of exhilaration at the prospect of changes which are supposed to lead to improvements. So much of their energies over the last fifteen years have gone into coping with the ever more urgent demands from government, funding councils and quality assurance bodies. They are the ones who have enabled a relatively small higher education system to grow into a mass system. They get little credit for it. So it will not be surprising if many of them do no more than pay lip service to the ILT and its doings.

However, middling and younger members of the profession are a different proposition. The cry for more discussion amongst peers, for the chance to watch one another at work is perhaps the most encouraging sign that the ILT has a rich future. They have their careers to worry about, they tend to see membership as an important badge of office which will contribute to it, and many of them are anxious to improve their contribution to improving the service to students. And they are nearer to students, the youngest of them recently having been students themselves.

- Enhancing the status of teaching
- Improving the experience of teachers
- Supporting innovation in higher education

They have much to contribute to realising that vision, all based on the search for improved learning and teaching services to whichever students they encounter. They are well placed to make it come about. The banality is true – in the longer term the future is in their hands. *They* will be the ILT. Where next? It all depends on how members manage to exploit the opportunities for promoting improvements in learning and teaching and reclaiming some of the fun, enjoyment and satisfaction which are the characteristic parts of teaching as a true vocation and profession.

Appendix 1 Accreditation and Teaching in Higher Education Planning Group

Membership

Chair	Professor Clive Booth
AUT	Dr Joanna de Groot
COSHEP	Professor George Gordon
CVCP	Professor Roger King
DfEE	Caroline Macready
HEFCE	Cliff Allan
HEFCW	Yvonne Hawkins
NATFHE	Ann Cotterell
NUS	Mark Grayling
SCOP	Dorma Unwin
SEDA	Carole Baume
SHEFC	Dr Paul Clark
QAAHE	Robin Middlehurst/Dr Vaneeta d'Andrea
UCET	Professor Ronald Barnett
UCoSDA	Professor Pat Partington/Professor Gus Pennington

Secretary: Patricia Ambrose

Project Officers
Jean Bocock
Dr Eric Macfarlane

Appendix 2 Institute for Learning and Teaching Planning Group

Membership

Dr Joanna de Groot (Vice-chair)	AUT
Professor Bill Stevely	COSHEP
Professor Roger King (Chair)	CVCP
Dr Robson Davidson	DENI
Cliff Alan	HEFCE
Roger Carter	HEFCW
Professor Roy Evans	HHEWNATRFHE
Norman Sharp	QAAHE
Dorma Unwin (Vice-chair)	SCOP
Dr Paul Clark	SHEFC
Professor Gus Pennington	UCoSDA

Observer:
David Burbridge	DfEE

Secretariat:
Patricia Ambrose	CVCP
Gerry Taggart	HEFCE
Greg Wade	SCOP

Appendix 3 Table 1

Category or level of membership	Illustrative range of responsibility
Associate Part One	Classroom practice; marking; evaluation of teaching.
Associate Part Two	In addition to the above: Design of a module, unit or series of teaching sessions. Design assessment, evaluation of modules.
Member	In addition to the above: Curriculum/programme design (e.g. across a degree); improvement of curricula/programmes; innovation in own course practice; evaluation of programmes; supervision of Associates.
Fellow	In addition to the above: Leader of change (across an institution or discipline) in teaching or curricula, through research, publication, work on disciplinary or professional bodies.

Appendix 4 Table 2

	Part One Associateship	Part Two Associateship	Membership	Fellowship
Planning	Plan teaching sessions	Plan a course within a current programme	Lead or undertake (re)design of a programme	Strategic planning. Develop policy led initiative
Conducting teaching and learning sessions	Conduct teaching sessions, using teaching and learning methods and C and IT appropriate to the particular circumstances of the discipline within the institution and the institutional setting and context.	Conduct a variety of teaching learning sessions and give pastoral and academic guidance, appropriate to the discipline and students, including designing, selecting and using appropriate learning resources and C and IT.	Provide a wide range of learning opportunities within specified teaching sessions. Use a wide range of types of teaching session. Design and create learning resources. Select, adapt and use appropriate C and IT. Develop/ redesign tutorial and guidance systems.	Develop an innovative teaching process. Plan new kinds of learning resources. Develop innovative use of C and IT.

Table 2 continued

	Part One Associateship	Part Two Associateship	Membership	Fellowship
Assessment	Mark and give feedback to students or assignments.	Design, implement and interpret assessment schemes and methods for a course (including appropriate use of self and peer assessment); give feedback to students on a range of work.	Design, implement and interpret assessment schemes and methods for a programme.	Develop new formative and summative assessment methods. Act as an external examiner.
Reviewing and improving teaching.	Review own teaching and plan to improve classroom practice.	Review range of teaching work and improve practice in a course, adapting to external changes and adopting appropriate innovations.	Review a range of teaching work and improve practice in a programme. Adapt innovations in academic practice for own use.	Review departmental teaching and learning practice. Create and disseminate innovations in academic practice.

Index